Blount reminds h
what he is doing
serious business;
He is taking it
breath is sealed off like placing a cork in a bottle; Hulm begins to inflate him with his own gases. Closer and closer. There cannot be much strength left in a ninety-four-year-old body. Blount applies himself to the task, the emotional edges retracting further. Harder and harder. In and out. Hulm flops on the bed. His body dilates. His eyes open and look into Blount's. In those eyes Blount sees his own face. He feels no horror. He looks no different than he has in years. Murder is not changing his features nor deforming them with complexity. It is now, it is always to be, it has always been the same old Blount.

Also in Arrow by Barry N. Malzberg

The Falling Astronauts

Barry N. Malzberg

THE MEN INSIDE

ARROW BOOKS

Arrow Books Ltd
3 Fitzroy Square, London W1

An imprint of the Hutchinson Publishing Group

London Melbourne Sydney Auckland
Wellington Johannesburg and agencies
throughout the world

First published in Great Britain by Arrow Books Ltd 1976

Made and printed in Great Britain
by The Anchor Press Ltd
Tiptree, Essex

ISBN 0 09 912820 9

This novel is for:
Harry Harrison, Robert Hoskins
and Robert Silverberg . . .
and for my parents.

"I will go into the core and, striking, take the sickness out. I will do this with humility because I am merely a Messenger. My enemy is metasteses, my cause their expulsion, my sin the vanity of pride, my future the casting of burdens for I am a Messenger . . ."

Oath of the Institute, 1996

"It's all a bunch of crap and don't you forget it."

Leslie Blount, 2022

1

In medias res, folks, here comes Blount. He is on the run and full of fun, looking for a follicle of cancer. Consider him if you will, if you must: his indignity, his power; he is twenty-two years old at this time, still and always-to-be virginal, sliding through corpuscles and strips of intestine like a beetle, scuttling through all of the fields of darkness. At the ready is his little lance, in his helmet is his tiny light, both ready to aim and cut. Think of Blount if you will: he is a man of some potential, education and background. Does he really deserve to be in a position like this? Mote in the crazed and sleeping Yancey, eighty-three years old and there he lies in the Institute at some enormous expenditure to be cured of his diagnosis. The figure for treatment bedazzles Blount; he continues on his way.

Deep in the bowels of Yancey, ladies and germs, tweezers held against his tiny eyes like a periscope, Blount now looks keenly for the cancer which he will eviscerate, drop into the pouch at his side and wing from the corpus of the patient. Nothing to this at all for Blount the friendly, local saint. In two hours Yancey will put tentacles on consciousness again, in two days he will recover mobility, in two weeks he will be released from the Institute, fifty thousand dollars lighter in assets but ready to resume that which he calls his life. Blessings for the disturbed Blount! he will do this for Yancey through his own effort, aided by the mechanism of the wonderful Hulm Projector the contemplation of which has given him so many happy hours. But Blount has problems.

This man has difficulties. Let us attend a shade more closely. He cannot find the site.

CanNOT find the site! disgraceful. The charts have located it precisely in the upper recesses of the colon, radiology and the fluoroscopes have pinned it within a millimeter of possibility but nevertheless Blount scrambles to a halt somewhere in that area and with the aspect of a man who has misread a timetable looks first one way then the other, his wee jaw dropping with astonishment. Into each life, even the happy life of a Messenger, some rain or blood must fall it would seem. Bad luck indeed for Blount: he cannot find what he seeks.

"Son of a bitch," our friend murmurs, talking to himself as Messengers are apt to do on and off the job, "I don't believe this. It isn't fair, how can they do this to me, where is that cancer?" Momentarily, staring at a kidney, he constructs a massive if rather schizoid explanation: there is no cancer. Or the charts have deliberately mislocated it. He is still in training, this is yet another test and supervisors are standing by the bed of the immobilized Yancey, following Blount's journey with micrometers and watching the bulging of the stomach. They are at this moment solemnly discussing Blount's control under stress and they are not pleased.

But Blount casts this aside as he has cast so much from him (not five years ago this courageous little fellow lived in Downside with a father who followed horses; if he can move beyond that then he can move beyond anything). The time of testing is over. He is a full-fledged Messenger now, Blount is. Two months duty in the Institute accomplished, diploma on the wall of his furnished quarters and Yancey is not his first case but his sixteenth. Fifteen successful eviscerations later the Institute would surely not be re-evaluating him; they have calculated their overhead down carefully the cheap sons of bitches, they would not waste the money observing a perfectly faithful Messenger. Nevertheless, where is that cancer?

Has radiology failed? Has this fool Yancey healed himself in the night? Was there never a cancer at all but merely an hysterical profusion of cells which Yancey, that religious fanatic, has shaken into quiescence? "Oh, this is too much," Blount reminds himself, articulate as always, master of the various mysteries of tongues. "Too much for me. I've got to find this obscenity thing. I can't stand it any more." He looks over the terrain again. He cannot find the obscenity thing.

Blount believes in the charts. He has learned to trust them, the little geometry of spaces which plot out his job and leave him with little other than the manual labor. The charts canNOT fail him now, any more than could the projector. (But if it did, Blount's present difficulties would go atwinkling; no, he will not even *think* of a failure of the projector.) In the Institute our dwarfish friend has learned faith; in the viscera of his clients he has learned application: surely, surely these excellent qualities acquired with such difficulty cannot fail me now. "Oh do not fail me now you sons of bitches," murmurs Blount, highly articulate even in this difficult pass and swings his gaze in increasingly wider arcs like the buttocks of a man fucking (what a scatological intelligence impotent little Blount has!) looking for a bump in the colon. Pity this man if you will: he is in deep trouble but he plods on, unaware of the calamities that await him, unaware of the fact that his troubles, in the truest sense, are just beginning.

Pinned in the colon, confused and irreligious little elf (otherwise he would attempt an incomprehending prayer) Blount sees healthy tissue, hanging and pulsating, all of this meat in the cavity. No hint of metasteses anywhere. Well, then, they have mislead him. Or Yancey has mislead himself. This is a healthy patient. The fluoroscopy has picked up phantoms, a false sign, rare but possible. This can be the only explanation. Blount inhales several gusts of foul body air through his five-eightieths of an inch frame, the air much like that in the kitchens of the Institute, feeling himself enlarge with pride. They will write him up in their journals after all. Five thousand Messengers in Institutes from Lisbon to the Dakotas perform their wondrous tasks in obscurity and only Blount to have dealings with a phantom-cancer. Extraordinary! Only twenty-two, he may be small but he is powerful. And now immortal.

He prepares to leave. It is really best that he do this because in fifteen minutes or maybe a little less than that the effects of the Projector are going to release and Blount, in or out of the cavity, is going to swell like a blowfish. He will grow from five-eightieths of an inch to his full and vigorous five-feet-one in the space of two-point-eight seconds *whoosh!* and if this process should happen to occur while he is still idly seeking disorder within Yancey's colon there will indeed be repercussions. Yancey will spatter; bits and pieces of the old millionaire will be all over the wall and hospital bed, a disgusting sight, bad for public relations and the laundry room to say nothing of Blount's future as a Messenger and nothing to be done about it no matter how demurely Blount would confront the Supervisors to point out that it could not possibly be his fault. It is definitely the time to get out of here; time is a-wasting as his father used to put it and so, another tired union worker who has not quite made shape-up, Blount tosses the little lance over his shoulder, adjusts the beam on the helmet to fullest intensity, and turns to trudge back wearily through the anal cavity to drop at last in a little gelid huddle on the sheets.

Disappointing, but Blount has the journals to bemuse him, along with a generalized feeling of relief. He has been spared a job after all and since he hates his job, a dirty, sweaty and disgusting detail performed upon patients most of whom he loathes, this is not to be derogated, not by the likes of this twenty-two-year old Messenger who is still working on the fourth month of the first year of his five-year indemnity.

"A job spared is still a piece of good time," he reminds himself, making up another of his spectacular aphorisms on the very spot of implication and then, as he gives one last checking glance, well—

—well, he sees the cancer after all, dead-center on the spot where it is supposed to be.

There it is! how could he have missed it? it is on the anterior wall in accordance with the maps, exactly where it must have been all the time that Blount was scurrying through his search. Did someone perhaps steal it and then replace it, smirking at Blount's discomfiture? Did it become reconstituted after a remission? Or did Blount miss the target because—leave it be said—he did not want to do the job and worked out a selective blindness? The possibility cannot be ignored. Blount is an honest man although limited in so many ways and if it is true that he would deliberately miss a site because he hated the patient or the job too much to function . . . well, then, he will have to discuss this with the Supervisors. In the meantime and absolutely no getting away from this now, he has to get the damned thing out.

Time's a-wasting: twelve minutes left on the Blount timer, glowing for miniaturized accuracy, now throbbing on his wrist. Twelve minutes in which to dig. There it is now, the bastard, dead before him, hanging as if suspended on a hook, faintly greenish against the red and black of the surrounding sections of the colon. It palpitates slightly like a fis in its element, frail little holes pinched into the sides further extending that piscine aspect, a haze coming off the surfaces like a religious aura and Blount, his lance already down into port arms position, approaches the cancer like a penitent. He falls before it to do his deeds. He falls to attack the altar of the cancer with the lance of the righteous and the reduced.

Blount is a religious fanatic, mildly-compensated: do not think ill of him. Anyone in his position must be so; do not think incharitably of this man. He is only twenty-three years old but most of the apostles were younger men. If he, if they, did not take the quest and personna at some level of symbolic inference, having, rather, to confront it strictly on what they call the reality level, Blount would be mad. He does not want to be mad; he cherishes his sanity, one of the last factors in his possession which connects him to the men outside.

There it is: eleven minutes left. Blount sets to work with a will, performs his horrid little tasks. As he works he sings to himself for comfort, anything for distraction at this time: he sings a popular song of the 1990's, the decade of his miraculous if hardly immaculate birth as he performs the necessary at a point of high remove. PATER NOSTER/COME FROM GLOUCESTER/ COME TO TAKE YOU AWAY?/GLORYA EXCELSIS/ IS WHAT THEY TELL US/SO WHAT YOU GONNA SAY? Blount sings cleaving, cleaving. BE GAY, BE GAY, BE GAY, COME WHAT MAY YOU MUST ALWAYS BE GAY.

Blount loves the old songs; they give him an apprehension of an era he but dimly grasps but suspects he would have been successful within, rather than the gray survival of his present maturity. If he had been full-grown in the 1900's, Blount likes to think, (how misguided he is) he might have invented the process himself, been like old Hulm; at the very least he would have gotten in early, near the beginning, might well be a director of the Institute now, sitting at a distance from the actual tasks, honored. Surely Blount would have been far-seeing enough to have backed old Hulm throughout the famous and early days of difficulty.

BE GAY, BE GAY. *Gloucester Retrieval*: top of the list in 1995 or was it 1996? either way before Blount's time, a good distance before. 1995 would have been near the heyday of his father who then forty-five would have been struggling with the first analyses of his maiden colts & geldings system, that system which was, no less, going to free the old bugger from Downside forever and bring him to the most perfect realization of all his purposes. *Gloucester Retrieval;* that was a simpler time all right, just as maiden colts & geldings was a simpler system. Following its first perfection came the second, third and fourth revivals during which this system was adjusted and readjusted by the aging Blount senior in accordance with the maneuverings of certain manipulative jockeys, trainers, officials & etc. which elements could not bear to allow the struggling Blount Senior, then going on forty-six, to construct a neat and infallable method of dealing with those factors which were crushing him out of existence.

Somewhat later on Blount's father got married, sired Blount, took Blount, abandoned his wife, not necessarily in that order and entered upon a Green and Blue Period during which all of the systems to which he was so dedicated were tossed into the waste pile and a newer approach was evolved, one of pure intuition: the naming of names, the coloring of colors. This system worked no better, really, than the Maiden Colts & Geldings method but it can be said again that Blount Senior found it easier to analyze horses this way and therefore the Green and Blue Period is not to be derogated. Do not discard it or anything else anent Blount Senior. Think of this distinguished sire as we see his tiny son, now twenty-three, bent over the task in a fury: like a man studying a racing form Blount's lips move and mumble as he applies himself to his work. WENT DOWN TO GLOUCESTER IN A FEVER OF NEED/LOOKING FOR THE SAVIOUR OH YES INDEED.

Blount is working on his sixteenth case now. He is still profoundly absorbed by the details of his work; it is only its politics which he is beginning to despise. Later,

Blount will become wholly cynical. His small, delicate frame will fill with dread and revulsion, he will decide that the actual act of the Messenger is as repellent as everything which leads on to the Becoming . . . but this is a bit in the future, one or two large days perhaps, even a week or so. For now, we can enjoy Blount just as he enjoys his work. Humming and slicing, Blout devotes himself to the mysterious cancer of Yancey, moving first with the chisel for crude cutting and shaping, then when the lump has been removed and secreted, coming in closer now, hand to hand, to do the fine work of taking out the metasteses piece by piece where it clings like a ghost to the nerve fibers. Yancey's blood is quickening with the thrill of relief, his respiration and gross motor functions accelerate. Blount sways gently in a bobbing breeze and holds on for support as he continues. He does indeed continue. Efficient and dedicated, this Leslie Blount. He is doing his work. One might even say that he loves it.

The spot has been localized. In range now with bare hands poised to grasp, Blount can see the gentle color of the dyes implanted. They glow orange in this deep cavity, sending forth a small corona or aureole which he much admires as he comes toward the center of his tasks. How could he have missed this cancer? What was wrong with him? Oh, it is a lovely one, beautiful! large and symmetrical, only slightly ellipsoid, almost circular, one of the nicest he has ever seen and one of the cleanest as well. It has spread but to no depth, Blount does not have to resort to surgical gestures in order to take all of it out. To the contrary, the cancer literally jumps into his hands, collaborating with him then in this act of extinction, surging from the fibers attaching with such ease that it seems to be doing a good portion of the work on its own. What a cooperative little tumor it is! Yancey for all of his age and decrepitude is of good stock and his overall condition is good. His body expels the cancer (with Blount's tricky assistance) as easily as the old man must have expelled the fifty thousand for treatment, right into the palm of the Institute.

Three minutes.

The timer booms for this, twitching Blount's wrist. A sharp twinkling is all that radar trace might pick up but in the amplification chamber of Yancey's corpus, it sounds like a muffled, terrible explosion (as it is meant to) shaking Blount's frame and he knows that it is now time to move. Three minutes to close up shop win or lose and take the commuter special out the anus, otherwise Yancey will have an unpleasant surprise. Blount moves in closer to the site, his intelligent, gnomish eyes seeking any suggestion of remainder. If he locates any it will be yanked out but quickly, quickly. His dedication is not all that it seems to be, however: his failure to clean out the spot will mean only that he will have to make this journey another day. Radiology will show traces of his failure; Blount has no desire to rent an evening's room again in the Yancey Projects.

But everything is clean. Nothing there: a small scar opening up through the colon, naked cells reassembling themselves in an indolent fashion like sunbathers coupling. The job is over. Two minutes. And a minute and a half. And a minute ten. And five. And four. The safety margin is a minute; the invitation to join us inside may not move below that figure for any reason, even a failure to clear the area. A pity to leave Yancey indeed but what is done is done and now the timer booms again. A minute now and it is time for Blount to abandon retrospect and popular song: he must move.

He does. he flings his lance back to right shoulder arms (there is something about the Messenger trade which is very military, and considering that Messengers are Drafted out of Downside this is perhaps fitting). He moves from the colon at a hasty, graceless trot, still humming the final bars of *Gloucester Retrieval* which he knows he will associate for the rest of his time with Yancey's colon, being still inexperienced enough in his work as to make emotional links. As to *need* those links. Up the colon and down the pipe; it would be better if Blount could make it straight through the colon, into the anal cavity and into the free if somewhat gusty air of the world but this route has been discussed and rejected in conference due to the age of the patient and the possibility that additional colonic irritation might lead to a recurrence of the complaint. Release forms or no, Yancey's interests would certainly sue. People with fifty thousand dollars no questions asked for surgery are not bound by release forms as poverty cases might be. Up and down the transective channels of the body Blout moves, shakes his head, clutches a hold for assurance, prays, prays some more, releases the hold, grasps again before disconnect and finally wills himself into release, bumpity-bumping his way through the large intestine, then like a man in a maze moves himself on hands and knees along all the coils of that intestine toward the true and open air. A circuitous route this, not to say a faintly disgusting corridor, but it is the safest. There exists in the annals of the Institute and one is taught about this early on, the tale of a Messenger who became confused in exiting and subsequently lost. He exploded his patient to a distance of thirty yards, a merry mess indeed but

He does, He flings his lance back to right shoulder

the Institute was at a more primitive stage in those times and since only late terminal cases were crazy enough to turn themselves over for work, there were few complaints.

This story may be apocryphal, Institute scatology to scare the recruits. Statistics were weighted against this kind of thing and the instructors were never specific about it . . . but it is to think about. Yancey would go off like a rocket. The approved angle of exit is against the large intestine, using its coils as a guide which must eventually, in forty feet or so even in the largest cases, lead to evacuation.

And so it does. It does again: small miracles of anatomy are worked over and again constantly in the work of Messengering. Say goodbye to Blount accordingly. He is going. He is gone. One last springing leap now and he will be lost from the angle of vision. Pay your very strictest and best attention to this little man now: you will not, all in all taken, see his like again and as he disappears at last it is with a gesture which might be one of dismissal or salute. Hard to say. Does not matter. He is gone. Blount is gone. Remember him with affection, for he has done his job.

Now, all is quiet in the Yancey Project. Murmurs of respiration, wicker of blood are part of the landscape like idiot birds cheeping in a field, crickets tuning for another dusk. Ignore them. Ignore the flickers of light and darkness passing through the great wheel of Yancey. No grinding of gears, no mumbles of popular song for the projects are once again and forevermore unoccupied. Loops and spires of intestine hang like trees swaying in the body's wind, the eighty-three-year-old heart beats on strong and true, transmitting the ruined blood. Light dwindles; night descends. All is well, for Blount—humble, cheerless Blount—is gone.

Gone and gone with him the cancer: the Yancey Projects will not fall into the sea. An unusual guest, Blount, he does not giveth but taketh away and what he taketh away is the greatest gift of all. Praise for Blount, then, this hardy little Messenger who, defying incredible odds to accomplish his spirited deed, is now perched half-size on the bed, vomiting as his own body extends. Blount does not know, good folks and true, how much more he can take of this.

2

In the twelfth hour, Yancey comes partially from the sedative block. He sees Blount in place, hovering there above his left shoulder. Messengers are to stay with the patients in the guise of male nurses through the early recovery period; it is best that the patient be exposed to as few people as possible—or so the Institute taught. Blount has a different idea: it saves on the overhead if the Messenger performs double-duty, intimate type. But is hard on the Messenger.

"There you are, son," Yancey says, speaking for the first time to Blount (he had been deeply drugged during their introduction), wrinkling and blinking on the sheets, "and there you are again. Seem to be two of you son; you seem to be drifting around the room a little and who are you anyway, bothering an old man in his last moments?"

"How do you feel?" Blount asks quietly. Of course Yancey is offensive. He is an old man, and a vain and wealthy one; Blount could have expected no different. Most of the patients at the Institute are disgusting. What did he expect? Blount reminds himself and counsels himself to be calm. "Do you feel all right?"

"What do you care, son," Yancey says with an intense and beatific smile, "how the hell I feel. You wouldn't know what feeling is. I am going to save your soul because you are irretrievably corrupt—you have explored the dark heart of corruption. Do you not know the evil you have touched, you little goon? Get out of my way; you're blocking the light."

Blount recoils slightly; he adjusts a professional demeanor ever more crudely across his features. "I only asked you how you were."

"That's none of your business," eighty-three-year-old Yancey, now empty of cancer says to him, "none of your affair how I feel—but how *you* feel, you dwarf: that is the question. Are you ready to face the nightmare within yourself? Are you ready to confront the seed of Adam which is pure and arching within you, driving you toward the greatest depths?" His eyes are as pure and white as the viscera was dense and clotted. Yancey is some kind of abusive fanatic.

That is all; Blount should be able to come to terms with this easily (he has dealt with worse) but looking at the old man, Blount feels his control waver. What is going on? What has happened to him? Is it circumstance? Motive? Or is Blount himself insane? The frail peripety to come will hinge on your choices; be circumspect. "I do not know," the imp, now again five feet one says, temporizing. "I really don't know what you're talking about."

Contact with Yancey has been slight. Patients come from the lower floors of this Institute already sedated (in more primitive days the Messengers had to drug them up as well but this was before Blount's time) and ready for entrance. They become personalities only in the stage of early recovery by which time, of course, it is too late to put the regrets into a practical format. "Rest now," Blount says. The block is removed only to test orientation for time, place and person, gross motor reactions; obviously Yancey is functional. He rummages for a hypodermic but unfortunately is not able to find one rapidly. Clumsy Blount! truly he has never had any luck.

"I will rest," Yancey says, "I will rest for eternity because I have faced God and have known Him and His wondrous works. My rest will be pure and deep, that is justice, but the question is, will *you* rest, you ugly little bastard? Do you too wish to enter upon that peace which passeth all understanding, or do you wish to delay the judgment to be rendered upon you?" His eyes blink but not with interrogation (this has really not been a question), hideous but placid against the sheets. Highly complicitous. "You must know, son," he says, "for these are questions you can no longer avoid and if it is necessary for me to shock you to win your fullest attention then so it must be for it is your slice of eternity which we are now measuring and we cannot be casual. Well, what do you think?" His eyes blink, but do not water.

Sedative block, open the lock Blount sings to comfort himself, trying to shut off Yancey, scrabbling away for a hypodermic. In aged, unstable patients like Yancey there are the possibilities of post-operative shock, unseen ganglia damaged, a failure of the CNS as yet undetected, and for that reason, the sedation must come off long enough for the Messenger to judge the orientations for time, place and person, long enough for him to check crude motor responses before injecting again the thalamic block that will quiet the patient for another six to eight hours. Repeating these notations to himself Blount finally, finally, finds the hypodermic, struggling with it fiendishly to load it up with the precious solution (do not laugh at this man; he is trying) and then, closing his eyes, throws three cubic centimeters of the precious solution into Yancey's system silently, struggling with the old man's arm as if it were a beam of wood or (horror!) a tumescent genital, pushing in the cubic centimeters to urge the old man toward silence and then with a whisk replaces the hypodermic within his robes like an assassin. So the robes, you see, are not ceremonial after all: they have a purpose. "Get me son," Yancey says; he twitches, mumbles, arches to the injection, and then closes his eyes. "Got me you crazy little obscenity but just wait a little more, I'll get you yet." He moans into unconsciousness. "Hail the redeemer," he says and is quiet.

Blount is alone again in the quiet post-operative room. He thinks of one thing and then he thinks of another. He mulls the present and then he considers the future. The past comes into play and he gives that worthy element consideration as well, humming and rocking himself above Yancey's sleeping form.

There is a great deal of time for his contemplations (which is good since Blount, despite a superficial articulacy, has quite a slow mind which forks its way to conclusions only as if pushing its tissue through gelatin) and he looks forward to all of it. He will be with the patient for the next forty-eight hours; he will have, then, ample opportunity to consider Yancey from every angle. Now and then he will have to make brief reports at the station down the floor and for what Blount delicately calls lavatory abuse, but these are on the periphery, what he will really be able to do is to look over Yancey post-operative and recuperative, pre-operative and doomed; he will be able to balance off the one thing against the other and also to interweave interesting and detailed reminiscences of his own, miserable, previous existence. Blount's Quiet Time then: the time which every Messenger is taught to cherish since it gives him the opportunity to Know His Patient. Oh, does Blount want to know this patient! He wants to know everything conceivable about old Yancey. Slowly, solemnly (no, his intelligence has never been of the quickening variety) he considers. Knowledge seeps into him, drop by drop, as pain would flood a wound. He considers many things.

He knows that he will have to kill Yancey.

3

See Blount years earlier: there he is in Downside. The travelogue has shifted from guided tour present tense to films of the past, to take you back personally to that wonderful and remarked upon year of 2017, a year never to be forgotten. The films are in excellent condition, the projectionist's booth is well-stocked: green and gold, red and blue, yellow and dense as the body's own artwork, these films will reveal all shades of meaning and inference so quietly in your places, folks, consider Blount's life. Not everything can be action, ongoing movement, there must be time to review the past which by all rights precedes the extant.

It is time that Blount's life be considered: someone must say something upon the subject of this daring elf because he did not reach this position idly nor is his life at all inconsequential. By measuring him, then, you may measure your own condition. Here is Blount in Downside: wicker of projector, flick of bulb, taking us back six years in time to that happier and more innocent period when the Colts and Militiamen were flying high in the American Division west and the newly inaugurated President was devoting himself, via pendant and crucifix, to the era of the new divine. Here is Blount, now seventeen again, discussing the events of the day lazily with his father.

"Mile and a furlong," says this extraordinarily old man, leaning forward more intensely into certain papers skewed before him on the bed, "mile and a sixteenth, forty-six and two fifths, got to go for the four horse then.

You see how it has to be the four horse, Leslie? The conditions here are absolute. But maybe I should cover the five, just to be safe. What do you think of the five? The hell with all this crap. It doesn't work. Nothing works anymore, they got it all tied down." Blount's father has not, to Leslie's knowledge, ever attended a racetrack in his life. All of his business is conducted through dead paper and the telephone; the sense of abstraction is infinite which may be the principle reason why Blount senior, in his forties and declining, is now utterly beginning to lose his sense of control. He cannot construct images for what they have been doing to him at these racetracks.

The film, as do so many of those made in the newer process, now accelerates, flicks back and forth in time, telescopes in one of those evasions of plot which have become fashionable. The old man stumbles from the bed, looks down upon the street, comes back to the bed, sits, stands again, moves toward the window, freezes this time. His activities are as circular as his condition. "What to say there, son? What to do?"

"What to do? Fuck you, that's what to do," says Leslie from his own pallet, lying in extremis with some pornographic photographs. He examines, has been examining, every detail of the male and female bodies intertwined in an act he will neither commit nor understand. Disrespectful tongue in this young man's head, not a shade of reverence in his bearing but he has lived with the old man for quite a while and thus may understand that love can be expressed only through connection on the proper level and, then, this is the way in which he will demonstrate affection for his father.

"Fuck me son? How?"

"Put those damned charts and systems away," Blount says, fingering himself to no sensation. "You're never going to get anywhere, haven't you faced that? You're just a bum."

"Yes," the old man says, turning from the window, laughing and cackling away, his amber-framed antique spectacles bouncing and jouncing on his nose as he approaches his son who does not put away the photographs at this gesture, nor attempt to conceal them in any way. "Yes, that is true, I am a total failure, you have found the truth of me, Leslie. But there must be something more. A man must keep on seeking something else, must strive beyond his background and those chains which encompass in the words of one or the other of our great leader." The words accelerate, actions speed, something has happened to the film for a great deal of time is now being jammed into a small reservoir of activity, foreshadowing Leslie's own occupational difficulties, of course. "Therefore," says the old man, dancing and prancing, "therefore, I am going to take you to the booth this afternoon, this very afternoon, and enroll you as a Messenger so that you unlike me may escape Downside to truly make something of your life."

Three months of dialogue, three months or more, seem to have been compressed into this single announcement but if the old man is conscious of this he does not seem dismayed nor discomfited in any way, except for certain twitchings of the extremities which can be ignored for now. Gross cerebral impairment comes on slowly; the old man has years left. "If you're lucky enough, that is to say, to get into the Institute."

"Lucky enough to get into the Institute!" Leslie shrieks. He springs at last, three months delayed, from his humble pallet and flings away the pictures in a lovely explosion of breasts, limbs and cavities. "Why you old bastard, they'll take anyone, anything *alive* in their Institute, how else do you think that they could ever stock them? I'm not going to be a Messenger," Leslie says piteously and inaccurately, making feeble attempt to leave the premises. "Just don't get any idea like bouncing me in there because I know what they do to people in that place and *I'm* not going to crawl into people to cut out their cancer. You think I'm crazy?"

"Yes, we think you're crazy," an usher comments through a megaphone, courtesy of the management, just to make the point absolutely clear. An unstable youth this usher and under no one's control (a relative of the manager) he is ejected immediately by an abashed and furious senior but too late, too late, the comment has been made. "Crazy!" the usher screams and a door slams behind; too late to redeem the comment.

Give Leslie credit. He does not overall submit to his strange and terrible fate but twitches and bitches a little as he slides all the way down. "I wouldn't get near that," the dwarfish youth says, opening his mouth to pant as he confronts his father, "why I wouldn't touch it with a pick. Get out of here, that's all I have to say."

"But you will touch it," says his old man, putting down the *Mocker Clocker* at last and turning his fullest attention upon the keen-eyed but slight offspring, the youth reacting to that attention in various degrees of defiance-and-submission which slowly reduce him to an upright position on the couch and then, with a sigh, supinity. Leslie has problems with his father: On the one hand he would genuinely enjoy patricide but on the other (a gentler phase which comes and goes by the pulse of the moon), he would settle for torture toward insanity, and the sheer alternation of these responses. Leslie's inability to decide exactly what he would like to do with his father given unexcelled opportunity is the major factor underlying his career and subsequent performance in different channels. "You will touch it and you will grow because, you see, we are going to a recruiting booth now."

Blount senior is determined and businesslike. The camera squares in showing the corners of his little mouth acquiring purpose, his small eyes peering now as if into great distance. "We're going to go down to the booth and see what we can do to get you out of the Downside and into the Institute; it's a rough trip, a rough proposal indeed son, not only for you but for me, to lose my only son and companion, but there's no reason why you've got to live like me, none at all. You can get something better to live for if you struggle. Every father owes this to his son, this I firmly believe Leslie and will not doubt it; owes to his son the small chance to get somewhere that the father wasn't and this for you is what I am going to do. Because I care and you're my cross to bear. But that cross is not my loss. Have no fear; I'm taking you there."

Poetic father! dialogue execrable. Do not take this production entirely seriously. The film is somewhat of a surrealist impression, less a factual and realistic summary then of Leslie's amazing career than any attempt to ram home to its higher and finer truth.

The film cuts to an exterior view and then as the camera reels back we are able to see for the first time the totality of Downside. Here it is: four square miles across, five hundred feet into the air in a series of uneven surges, and deep, miles and miles down to the gray center of the Earth. Multicolored haze shifts through this landscape: deep in this haze can be seen staggering forms, machinery pumping, idle zephyrs chasing paper and dust about and as the light comes on fully Downside brightens, painted in colors of red and green, stretched from river to river in a narrow strip, clutching at the rivers with arms of drowned land, drowned lover. Through these spaces Leslie and his father now prowl, gait between a scuttle and flight.

On their way to the recruiting booth of the Hulm Institute, the father in the lead, the dwarfish but brilliant youth following somewhat sullenly, casting glances of potential flight left and right but not fleeing, so tied is he to his father, the old man leading the way quietly, confidently, a new spring in his horseplayer's step as he proceeds toward the place of appointment. On this journey

Leslie and his father witness: four assaults, two murders and one gang of police placing incendiaries. This does not represent artistic compression but indeed an accurate representation of routine events as part of an unremarkable day in Downside, neither to be remarked upon or avoided . . . although the brush of one murderer's bullet comes rather sickeningly close to the well-chiseled and highly attractive left ear of Leslie who was barely aware of his perilous edge on death until he had fallen off it. Firearms by common decree are carried by almost all of the residents of this area so that all disputes may be settled on the spot. The police incendiaries, however, may be considered to be of an optional nature, being planted only when in the judgment of rather reluctant authorities, local disturbances threaten to spread over a larger area and the spot of trouble, therefore, must be sealed off.

Leslie and his father, righteously enough, do not carry guns. Blount senior believes that weapons in the hands of the inexperienced only increase danger but now, his glance sweeping nervously to the left and right, the forward and the back of him, Leslie is not so sure that his father's policy was correct nor, for that matter, that the errand to the recruiting station should have been taken so lightly. One does not venture into these streets with casuality, even if one is merely seeking a way out.

Blount senior, however, has the invulnerability of the truly insane. He proceeds on the point with the dumb conviction of a saint and somewhat awed by this (and fearful as well because he is beginning to believe that Blount senior may be the only mobile decombatant zone in the area) Leslie follows, closing up the gap between them as they move on so that by the time they come to Pennsylvania Avenue and the turnpike underpass, Leslie is walking in virtual filial embrace with the old man, cultivating a closeness which they have not had in many years. "You see what I mean?" the fine old man says as a tank goes *clank!* on the turnpike above, cannisters of poison gas jangling merrily as it passes down the line, taking an access road to Downside. "You see what the story is with this place? You've got to work your way out of it, Leslie: this is no place for a fine boy. Got to get out and the Institute can show you the way. There's the booth; the booth's right up there and so it is, your gateway to a better life," pointing, motioning, and indeed the alert old man has told him true. For once his information proves to be completely accurate and the two Blounts, father and son, stand *al fresco* in the corridor of Pennsylvania Avenue, looking at their Gateway to a Better Life while derelicts and murderers, slattern and homeless children scatter to and fro about them, croaking their affirmation and not a one, not a single one even gives the Gateway a look-see.

Is this, then, an indication of Blount's fate? Does the isolation of the booth mean that palpatating waves of dread coming from the boy are so tangible that even a resident of Downside knows enough to stay clear? Or does it indicate, more simply, the relation that the Institute bears to Downside, the cunning of those residents being more than sufficient to protect themselves from such inducement.

Blount and his father, now striding side by side, six-feet-two of decrepitude, five-feet-one of boundless energy, fling open the wooden door and stroll their way into the booth where they are greeted by odors, darkness, cries of salutation, leaflets, pummelings, music. Other trumpetings: from behind the desk, wearing the approved dress uniform of the para-military Institute, the symbol of the Hulm Projector blending in neatly with the cloth and wallpaper of the booth containing that very identical symbol, the recruiter hurls himself upon Blount and his father.

YES SIR, he says, HAVE YOU COME TO BRING THIS BOY IN HERE TO BE A MESSENGER? SIT

RIGHT DOWN AND I WILL GET THE PAPERS TO FILL. WHAT CAN I TELL YOU ABOUT THE INSTITUTE? WHAT COULD I ADD OF THE CRAFT OF THE MESSENGERS? AN UNPARALLELED OPPORTUNITY, YOU HAVE MADE A WISE DECISION FOR THE BOY, SIR, AND YOU TOO, YOUNG MAN, ARE FORTUNATE TO HAVE SUCH A FATHER ALTHOUGH I CAN SEE BY YOUR RATHER SULLEN EXPRESSION THAT YOU DO NOT QUITE BELIEVE THIS. YOU WILL, YOU WILL. ONE MOMENT AND I WILL GET ALL OF THE FORMS TO PROCESS YOU IN. WOULD YOU LIKE TO ENJOY A TRAINING FILM WHILE YOU WAIT?

"No thank you," Blount senior answers, fitting his palms into tight alignment along the desk and leaning forward with steel cunning. "That will not be necessary. The boy is already very familiar with the material and is much interested in determining an enlisting. He's the proper height, isn't he?" Senior's rhetoric has gone a bit askew under the pressure but he continues trying for elevation. "He wishes to join the ranks of the traditional Messengers," he adds, "and is of the proper height, will you not tell me?"

OH YES, HE IS INDEED THE PROPER HEIGHT, beams the recruiter, scuttling, averring, reaching inside the desk to emerge with variously colored strips of paper which he sifts before them, looking frantically for a pen. THE SUPERFICIAL INDICATIONS ARE VERY GOOD: THE ONLY PROBLEM WILL BE AGE VERIFICATION; THE BOY MUST BE OVER SEVENTEEN SO THAT WE CAN BE POSITIVE HE HAS REACHED ALMOST HIS FULL GROWTH. DISAPPOINTING TIMES IN THE PAST, WOULD YOU BELIEVE THIS, WE HAVE HAD PEOPLE COMING IN WITH YOUNG CHILDREN, CLAIMING THEM TO BE NEARLY ADULTS. BUT THE BOY'S FEATURES LOOK VERY SETTLED, I AM QUITE

SURE THAT HE IS OF AGE AND IF HE CAN PASS THE QUALIFICATIONS—

Now the camera pans in as it has a tendency to do every now and then; most of its shots have been at medium-mix, showing the characters perched in the manner of still-lives, in rather bleak relationship to their environment, Downside being hinted in a series of angles and sweep-shots which may indicate only the ineptness of the director . . . but now, as the camera dives close the film takes one of its rare portraitures. We see the eyes of the recruiting Messenger in stark relief against the screen, peering, expanding to fill most of its area.

Green and blue those eyes are, not unlike the shadows of Downside. They are filled with their own intensity and penetrating more deeply we can, as if for the time, see a hint of incipient madness. A strange, discolored light vaults and leaps from the eyes, it is this which makes cross-connection with Blount and for an instant the two of them, the camera now reeling back a little, stare at one another over the hum of the machinery.

Blount and the recruiter, the recruiter and Blount, trade a look both above and below the level of connection and then settle for ferocity. In the eyes of the recruiter, it may be deduced, Blount sees himself but that is too obvious for the ambitious film director who is obviously trying to indicate that the recruiter in Blount also sees an image of what he once might have been . . . but instead of bringing them together more closely this look, rather, seems to wedge them apart. It is not a joining but a separation as insight so often is and from the exchange of too much perception they turn them from one another, Blount to consider certain postage signs and clippings on the walls, the recruiter to stare at the form.

EXACTLY THE RIGHT HEIGHT the recruiter says again but this time with a sigh, the capitalization beginning to ease, the speech remitting to the old green and gold of Downside. "I'm sure that he'll fit into our schedule quite well and he happens," the recruiter says, "the boy just happens to be coming in at an excellent time now sir, there are some interesting vacancies, fascinating vacancies made available. A good time, a good time sir to join the corps."

The shift is clear. The recruiter feels that in that exchanging stare he has lost the enlistment and now he must participate in his disgrace; he must observe Blount slowly moving from him, the father quite helpless to prevent the flight of the nearly betrayed but narrowly saved youth.

He has misjudged Blount's father, though, and the relationship which these two have had together. It is an old mistake. The recruiter is not the first to have made it.

"Yes," Blount says. He does not flee toward the door at all but rather retracks to pick up the forms, "yes, many fine opportunities, just the right height, good time to come in, good time for Messengering." The lad's spirit is quite whipped and beaten you see (otherwise, how could his father have gotten him there to begin with? and in the bargain it has been quite a solemn stroll through Downside for Blount; he does not want to remain here, he will admit this). "Just give me a pen; I'll sign anything."

"Are you of age, son?"

"This boy is seventeen" says Blount senior, "and surely that makes him of age, doesn't it? If not, I'll sign for the lad; just give me the pen. A great thing, a great thing, I told him that it would be the key and the gateway to the future for him."

"Have you a birth certificate?"

"In my wallet," says Blount senior, not to be outmaneuvered and produces a slip of paper indicating the Nativity of Blount. "Here it is; had it all the time. I want this to be a clean enlistment for the lad. I'm an honorable man."

"Of course you are," the recruiter says, looking carefully at the certificate and nodding his head. "I can see that. I never meant to impugn your motives; it's just that every now and then—"

"There are dishonorables in Downside," Blount senior comments, "the area has retrograded significantly in the last few years. Still, there are some of the older stock people such as myself who believe in the concepts of honor and the responsible."

"When am I going to begin training?" Blount says. "The sooner the better if you don't mind."

"Well, son," the recruiter says rather speculatively, the shock of the exchange still within him, taking a careful line then, "that all depends. You can start your training in the new October session which will be forming within the next two weeks and go right into the preliminaries or, if you're really eager, we might be able to work you into some kind of a special section, a layover so to speak, so that young lads like yourself will be able to begin at once by studying the lore and science of the Institute. That means that when the regular sessions start you'll have a lead on everyone." The recruiter suppresses a surprising giggle. "A head start on all the others, you see, so that what they'll be *learning* you will already *know* and this will speed you through your courses and possibly make you a candidate for acceleration which would give you your drill in just three and a half years. This isn't the usual procedure of course but if you qualify for the program it's good because you'll still be credited for four years in the Institute which means that although you are on a standard seven-year enlistment you'll actually only be in for six and a half which is highly desirable."

"Is it?" Blount senior says, "I wouldn't hurry the boy out; I think he'll enjoy it."

"Of course he'll enjoy it," the recruiter says rather frantically, "I didn't mean that he *wouldn't* enjoy it. But good time is good time and a half a year early out means more money for him sooner on the re-enlistment." He tries to wink, an eye becomes palsied, he clasps his hands to his face (the film has speeded) and falls sighing to his chair. "Please, sign the forms sir if you will," he says to Blount's father.

"I'm about to," the old man says, "just about to; had it in mind every step of the way, now," and brandishes the pen in his hand, the very pen that the recruiter has clipped inconspicuously to the forms, "but before I do I have a question."

"Yes?"

"It's an important question but I'll come right to the point. I am not a man to circumlocute when time can be saved by directness."

"I should say not."

"When do we get the bonus?"

"Ah," the recruiter says. "Ah. The bonus."

"It's on the spot, isn't it now?" The old man's eyes narrow with mad cunning. "That's what the bulletins said. On the spot."

"Well, there are certain procedures—"

"Produce the bonus and you have yourself a fine lad, one that I'm looking forward to as much as you, the news of his accomplishments. I give to you my only son—"

"There are, as I say, procedures—"

"On the spot," says Blount senior. "After all," he adds, now holding the pen before his teeth, stroking that pen gently but decisively as if it were a sexual implement which it is distinctly not (both the producer of this film and its protagonist being quite puritan), "that was the set of terms I understood to be offered here."

"Well, it's not quite on the *spot*. The posters might give that impression; it certainly can be close to immediate but everything depends, sir, upon whether or not this boy may qualify. He will qualify; I have no doubt of that, but the ratio of acceptances, unfortunately, is not *absolute* and until the preliminary checks have been completed to clear some hidden pattern, some psychic abhorrence to the position—"

"Then I won't sign," says Blount senior, chuckling grimly for the cameras, conscious of them for the first time and now playing up for the focus. "There's not a chance that these forms will be signed until you settle on him. That is the method of the announcements and I will not have this lad cheated out of his rightful bonus on a technicality."

"Ah," says the recruiter, "aha, aha," his little insignia palpitating on his chest as his breath loses some of its regularity, "aha, uh, the bonus, yes indeed but it is the property of the enlistee's to make disposition and the check, the check would have to be made out to the young man in any event although I know that you have his best interests . . ."

"Any disposition I make will be acceptable to him. Won't it, Leslie? He's a fine lad, he listens to his old father, he knows the trust we have in one another and the important thing is to get him into the Institute and away from these terrible streets, this very dangerous section. He's a gentle boy; he's not ripe for Downside, he must be protected."

"Leslie," the recruiter says, addressing Blount in a seemingly confidential way, "do you *want* the bonus settled? Wouldn't it be more reasonable to wait until the tests have cleared? You'd only have to refund it if you proved to be insufficient."

Well, furthermore. The camera comes in closely upon Leslie. This is his key moment of the sequence, his central peripety from which will spring all of the narrative and he knows this no less than the two other principals. Nor is he unequal to the task. Leslie has never been unequal to any of the tasks which have been so gracelessly imposed upon him; this is one of the various feeder lines connected to his greatness. There are others. We will see them presently. Now, five years back, he casts shy, seventeen-year-old Downsider's eyes to the floor, scuffles seventeen-year-old size four shoes upon the floor, blushes and seems on the verge of spitting but thinks differently of this and instead ingests sputum without difficulty. "I'll do anything," he says, "that my father tells me to do," using the wispiest of little voices here (but no effeminacy in it: Blount is not effeminate but vigorously masculine; he chooses not, for personal reasons to enact his masculinity), "if he says that I won't sign until the bonus comes through then that's all right and if he wants to sign it now that part's all right too because it's all up to him. I'll go along; I have nothing to say about this matter."

He coughs, grumbles, clears his throat quietly. He is still the focus of attention: his father and the recruiter look upon him now, his father with the largest and kindliest eyes Blount has ever seen in that introspective face. Blount speaks! He announces himself; he stakes out a position! For the first and possibly the only time in his difficult career to date, Blount expresses himself at length, allowing his philosophy, his personna, to lunge forth. He knows that what he has said is not yet sufficient to the occasion; he knows that more yet needs to be said and so he continues.

"You see," Blount says, keenly, carefully, turning in upon himself as it were so that the inmost core may be known, "you see, I really don't like this place. I want to get out; the average age in Downside is about fifteen, making it to thirty is a real accomplishment, my father has to have been great to make it to forty-five and frankly I don't want to die."

"I put it all on the horses, boy," Blount senior says proudly, "they have kept me young and off the streets."

"But I'm not interested in horses. There must be something else and if the only way that I can get out of here is to be a Messenger, that's okay with me. I don't want the bonus or praises, I just want out. I really do want to get the hell out," Blount says mildly enough, kicking at something on the floor. His eyes rear then to the ceiling, his hands snap to a prayerful posture and this, folks, well this—

—should be the end of the scene by all rights and in fact it is, this film being surrealistic only when necessary and it is quite necessary now. This film is of highly symbolic important because its scenes and juxtapositions are abbreviated rather than carried toward their most logical extension. And so, now, the recruiter and Blount senior fall upon the lad with anxious cries; they encircle and embrace him, their faces bent toward him in gestures both vampiric and affectionate and Blount seems to disappear under this tumble of arms and legs, pelted as he is by hailstones of praise. Emotion has overtaken this old man; he blabbers with passion and beckons his son against his breast.

"But I really *do* want to get out of here," Blount says quietly again, "that's what I meant to do, to get *out*." Really, he does want to get out of Downside. Blount kicks at something on the floor; his eyes rear toward the ceiling, his hands snap to a prayerful posture (you have seen this already but be patient) and once again Blount senior and the recruiter fall upon the lad, embrace and encircle him, their cries like hailstones in ascent and descent, plunging in and out of this scene with a sexual lust and inquisitiveness and then coarse, thick walls slam down on the point of view and there is no more. An intermission break has been signaled.

Oh yes indeed: even Blount must have an intermission, an intermission of the soul if you will, please leave your seats quietly and in good order, without panic but with the necessity to clear the theater at once for cleaning and the search for implanted incendiaries. There are refreshments available at modest cost in the lobby to keep you occupied, refreshments and souvenirs of

Blount's occupation as well for your amusement and amazement. You will find in the lobby at a very reasonable price models of his little lance and prowling shoes, you will find models of the intensely valuable Hulm Projector (protected by interlocking patent) available for your inspection, you will find facsimiles of Blount's lecture notes and laboratory exercises as compiled by the eager and dedicated youth through his four long and dedicated years in the Institute—

—for it is intermission time and all your needs (as Blount's cannot) will be satisfied in the access to the lobby. Leave quietly. Leave quietly, please. No jostling in the aisles. No pushing against one another or idle threats of violence in the rush for space: cancer may be growing in any of you out there and it is best not to stimulate terminal conditions. The treatment is enormously expensive.

Blount could perform his wonders upon you too if he would but it will cost fifty thousand dollars, payment in advance, no guarantees and there is not an insurance company in the world which would provide policy protection. Take those rear exits, drink your orange drink in the lobby, leave the auditorium vacant ladies and germs so that Blount himself—oh, this operation is run on a very tight budget!—may be left briefly to himself, sobbing and clutching in the projectionist's booth, trying to splice on a new reel.

4

Blount knows that it will be hard to kill Yancey. There are not only certain laws of the Institute and society against such matters, he is not sure if at the last moment some frail spurt of reluctance will cause him to desist. Also, how will he do it? by lance or by fire, face to face or by pulling the plug on the old man in the middle of the night? Does he want to get caught or doesn't he? Would he like to make a statement to the press after arraignment or would it be better if the old man's death were listed *inevitable* (ten percent of patients, after all, *do* die before they can be released) and Blount continues on his merry way? He does not know; he really does not know. *Apprehension is justification*; Blount is aware of this, but then too the prisons are apt to be colder than Downside.

He is deeply convinced of the necessity, the sheer goodness of the act, Blount is, but then again he has no relationship with Yancey so far and murder would have to be an irrelevancy. He can feel the murder inside him, create a network of inferences of how it will feel to do it (will it feel fine? he thinks so) but in the absence of hard information, specific facts, details of the character and personality, what would it accomplish at this time? Would Blount learn from it; would he grow? Would he come from the experience a larger man? (In spirit that is to say; physically Blount has reached his limit.)

He must know more about Yancey, that is all there is to it.

Necessary to consider Yancey: the pre-operative informational is even barer then usual and more direct confrontation must be sought. The idea of the informationals was always a good one; a pity then that the Institute has so deserted important original insight. Back in 2008 or so, when the first policies and procedures in the conglomerate framework were being hesitantly assembled, old Hulm himself, then seventy-nine years old and in the full bloom of his senility, had ruled, taking command of a board meeting, that a Messenger must Know His Patient. Mere willingness to trot into the intestines was not enough when dealing with cancer; the Messenger would be even more likely to take the anal leap if there were a feeling of *personal involvement* . . . so that there would be even less inclination to allow a stray fiber to lie there ominously if the Messenger felt that he was dealing with a friend, rather than a body draped under a sheet. "Leave it be that way," said old Hulm and that way it was left; Hulm issued all the commands and dictums until 2015 when a severe stroke disabled the dynamic old founder of the process and put him on his deathbed. He has been on his deathbed for eight years now, always with vigor.

But at that time the control was absolute; now it has diffused to thieves and distant relatives (Hulm had no spawn) and long biographies were compiled, pre-operative interviews, long sessions at the patient's bedside in which dreadful confidences were exchanged. It was a policy offering the patient and Messenger the greatest of mutual rewards . . . except that certain influential patients began then to resent not only their viscera but their indelicacies being mapped out on a series of charts and therefore the policy, alas, is not what it used to be although it is still paid its regards. Regards by the Institute are paid all fragments of its history as it staggers into the future: like flies on meat, these Messengers gird their tiny loins to prepare, into the breach good friends, to do battle with the Big C.

So Blount knows little of Yancey; all that he knows at this moment, in fact, is that the old man is eighty-three and until a few hours ago doped to the gills from admission-time due to the great amount of pain. Occupation retired. Nearest and only living relative: Susan Forks. Susan Forks: granddaughter, age twenty-three, unmarried, resident with Yancey at his address in Platte. Incest, then? Or some other mad convolutions of eighty-three and twenty-three which sought mask by a constructed relationship? Blount's muddy little mind scuttles through this point: it is certainly hard to tell, it need not concern the impotent but agreeable Blount whose considerations on matters sexual have always been of marginal facility. Was Yancey then industrialist or derelict, retired evangelist or madman, cheerful, sated acceptor of his sins or fallen to commit new ones? none of this, alas, revealed in the few paragraphs printed out for the sheet handed Blount and no conversations before the fact of the operation either.

No, no such luck for Blount: Yancey lay like an algae on that bed, palpitating faintly, murmuring through tubes in his nostrils. Poor enough basis for those expected intimacies but Blount did the best for him anyway, Blount has always done his best, no one will understand this, and where oh where has it taken him? What has Blount's sacrifice, the dedication of this hard-working Messenger earned him? oh it is not fair.

Yancey will have to be killed. Blount is serious. He means this. He is not talking through his teeth. He will do it and the singing vault of the undetectable murder (for Blount is not saint enough to murder careless of apprehension) will change him into a new person; Yancey's spirit, at the instant of death, will transfer to Blount's in a *whoosh!* and it will be as if Blount's little soul, expanding from one-eightieth of an inch to five feet one in a period of minutes, will acquire an entirely different perspective on the world. He will murder Yancey to eat of his heart.

But now, at this instant, Blount is in a tragic but simple rage. Yancey is only his sixteenth case; he is still new enough to the trade, you see, to take it all personally and he is driven to understand what he has done, no matter how slender the informational basis. How could Yancey be killed otherwise? Blount has gone into his rear with the blessings of the Projector, seeking to pluck the cancer from him like a pitted prune, the least that he could do is to have had relationship with the custodian of the vitals. (The man really thinks this way. He truly thinks in exactly this fashion.)

No. He will, he resolves, have no matter of it. He will go to the floor supervisor, Blount will, and will cunningly obtain pieces of information on the patient by feeding that nurse offhand questions and soon he will learn everything that is necessary to kill him. If this does not work (but it must) Blount will write a letter to old Hulm himself, blessed Hulm, ninety-four years old and only in partial coma, as vigorous as he was three years ago, not a hint of decline in his stabilized condition the wonderful old geezer and let Hulm know that his own policies are being defied.

HEY, Blount will write, HEY, HULM, CONTRARY TO YOUR OWN POLICIES AND PROCEDURES, WE ARE BEING DENIED DOSSIERS ON THE PATIENTS. WHAT DO YOU INTEND TO DO ABOUT THIS? I AM TAKING THE COMPLAINT TO THE VERY TOP BECAUSE I MUST ESTABLISH A RELATIONSHIP WITH A MAN I AM ABOUT TO MURDER. YOURS VERY TRULY, BLOUNT.

Would this letter work, the swarthy but handsome youth wonders. No, it probably would not work.

Leave it for later, no need for letters now. Wandering down the hall to take up post by his patient once again (Messengers are allowed fifteen-minute breaks every two hours, is this not wonderful? they may use the lavatory, meal facilities, enjoy rest and recreation), his elfin limbs oiled by fatigue to splendid coordination, Blount passes: nurses, attendants, physicians, ambulatory patients, conversational huddles, laboratories and runs into, almost toppling, the granddaughter of Yancey himself. Susan Forks. Susan Forks backs into a wall, her face assorting itself into lines that might be furious until she recognizes and then all of the feeling drains from that face, passes through her neck and settles into her stomach, pulling her down to an instinctive crouch. An athletic and precise girl. "Hello," she says. "It is you, isn't it?"

"Certainly," Blount says with assurance. It is the second time they have met. Susan brushes hair from her forehead absently, looking down at Blount's little rubber shoes. "Is everything all right with him?"

"Certainly everything's all right."

"Well, I thought so. I mean, there's no reason why it shouldn't be; I was just in there and he looks fine. Very strong." Is it possible Blount wonders that this is dissembling, that the girl is covering up her own anxiety for Yancey to die in order that she may inherit the old bastard's money? It is a possibility. "Very strong," she says meditatively, and presses one palm against the other palm, *whikk!* as she brings clasped hands over her head, exposing her breastline to the unstimulated youth. "He's even talking," she says vaguely, "religious stuff, not making much sense. Well, that's my grandfather."

That is indeed her grandfather. Look at her, imagine her huddled in bed with Yancey, those two bodies, gray against the background, sixty years separate in time and space, swaddled by need. Yancey's splintered flesh against her smoothness, huffings and jumpings, pumpings and puffings in the corridor. Why not? More unlikely things have happened.

"Don't worry about his condition," Blount says, double-edged, "everything will work out, I'm sure."

"Are you?"

"Of course, of course. The treatment is all coming along nicely. Tell me something about him," Blount says taking her arm, the touch metallic under the clothing, guiding her down the halls assuming intimacy, "he must be a very interesting man; he's told me a lot of things already. Would you like to tell me about him?"

"I have to go now," Susan says. "I just stopped by the hospital to see him, but I don't have time—"

"All right," says Blount. They are at the door to Yancey's room; peering he sees an image of the old man lying as if he were in his coffin, "if you don't want to talk, don't talk. I'll go back to him."

"No," she says. "No, wait." Her eyes moving in a slow arc, halting, pressing against Blount, shocking contact, her breasts come into play like little lances against his chest, her eyes open. "Wait, I must tell you something. I need your help."

"Help?"

"Yes," she says, leaning over the little lad and miming a gesture which might be a bite of Blount's ear. "Help me decide what to do."

She brushes a hand down Blount's arm; he feels pressure, lifting. The girl must be mad; she has become overcome by insistence. "Come here," she says, taking the Messenger by a palm, leading him over to a wall; they pass through corridors then, doors open like abscesses upon sleeping patients, crumpled patients, ambulatory patients, some of them in for operations, others merely in the exploratory phase, whisks him past Yancey's cubicle and finally then at the end of the hallway, jammed against a window which looks out from the fourth floor upon the city, haze billowing in the dead air, blocking the view of Downside which sprawls four miles to the south (Blount hopes that he will never see it again), presses his hand again, leans forward intensely, mimes the gesture of biting Blount's little ear again and says to him, flatly and with perfect seriousness and Blount is sure that he is hearing this because he has always trusted his senses although he has not precisely enjoyed them, "Do you think that you could kill him?"

And hangs there in frieze for a while, camera holding to still and steady angle while her little eyes dart and flash and then, she asks again, as to be assured that she has said it, "I want you to kill him."

For the moment, Blount hears no more.

5

Later, in the brisk sleep granted him, Blount has a dream and in this dream Yancey stands before him fully restored, youthful in his eighty-three-year-old body, vigorous, transcendent of cancer, looking at Blount with eyes wise and compassionate, twisted with the pain he has known but careless of it. "I only wanted to help you son," the dream-Yancey says with enormous calm, "only wanted to save you from your own corruption, don't you know that?" He squeezes Blount's arm, winks confidentially. "A dirty job, a dirty job," he sings, "climbing into an old man's belly, twirling your way through an old man's vitals, it can do terrible things to a fine young man, fill that young man with a sense of decay. I wanted to save you that, don't you realize? I wanted you to become clean and purified in the fire of God. All of us are the children of God, son; I wanted you to accept that divinity."

Yancey touches him again then in a gentle and reassuring manner as Blount, weak in this dream and not in the manner of himself collapses before Yancey moaning. "Help me, help me," the collapsed Blount is saying, "can't stand this anymore, you've got to help me," and Yancey, wise and strong, hovering above him says, "I will, I will help you son, I want to help everyone because I have been restored."

Blount feels the power coming from Yancey, the power comes off in thick oozing waves that seem to lift the little Messenger above himself, hovering at some height in the air he looks down upon Yancey transcendent, transfixed, the old man opening his mouth to say the words that will finally liberate Blount totally from his corruption, and from the image of the gut he has prowled, but just as Yancey begins to speak the dream collapses in a clash of static and wiring and Blount, lunging from the chair, finds the old man strangling in his tubing on the bed and has to struggle frantically for a moment to clear the breathing passages so that this shrunken and real Yancey will not die on the spot for him—depriving Blount of the murder. Depriving Blount of what surely must come but only by his own hand. Confused and pained in the peculiar way in which only he can be, Blount settles himself by the bed again and wills himself back to sleep. But the dreaming will not come and in the collision of empty colors before his consciousness, Blount realizes that he will never touch this aspect of the old man again.

6

2021, brief lunge in time (as Blount must make brief lunges from his chair every now and then to assure that Yancey will not struggle): it is the night of the graduation, Blount has completed his studies at the Institute. In one hand he has been given a tiny drill, in the other a diploma; against his chest he has clutched the robes of the Institute bearing the fresh insignia of the Messenger. Now it is somewhat later; this triumph behind him, Blount has gone solitary to the Arena, there to forget his troubles with a spot of relaxation. Blount does not know the rituals of celebration; he has voyaged alone, had too much to drink, refused drug assistance, denied the offers of women who, for a small fee, would deprive him of his virginity; now he stands reeling against a wall somewhere in the bowels of the Arena, trying to focus his vision and understanding that he may faint at any time. Next to him stands an attendant; a middle-aged woman. She has already made a sexual offer to Blount, been denied; now she stands at his service, a look of discontent alternating with passion on her face in the best mode of the Arena. She seems bored but then again fulfilled; the Arena will do this to its employees.

"What do you want?" she says. If only she knew! "What do you want? Maybe you should go home, son: it's getting late."

"I want a Priest," Blount says with the ponderous certainty of the truly insane. "Lead me to a Priest."

"A confession machine?"

"I don't know what you call them here; I thought they

were named Priests. Whatever it is, lead me to it. Lead me to a Priest right now," the small lunatic says now, seizing the attendant by the robes and yanking them like a child. "Please," he says, his mood shifting to wistfulness with the ability of the mad, "get me one."

The attendant looks at Blount, a hint of puzzlement mingling with fatigue on her tired face. Blount, with his new clinical interest, detects a fine, brown wart that will flower to cancer in five or six years with luck; thinks that he can see under the skin to the filaments it will cast. Burn it out fast and horrid with a deep knife if she is lucky; otherwise some Messenger might have to go inside her cheek. She fingers the wart as if there has been some transfer of energy there. "You see," she says, "we don't hear many requests for the Priests these days."

"No one has anything to confess?"

"Maybe not. Not the way you think."

"*I* want to confess," Blount says. He is a Downsider; feels the stain of his guilt now radiating as if in spokes. "I need to." He is fascinated by the attendant's wart. Very well then, he will not look at it. He will depersonalize. It is enough that she has offered, for a fee, to fuck him; he does not have to think of her warts. "Get me there."

"It's not working too well you see. There isn't too much demand."

"You said that."

"Well, there isn't! We have an old one on hand just in case but the gearing is wrong. Something to do with the circuits . . . I don't think that you'd be very happy with it."

"I'll take my chances," Blount says. He dances and prances a little in place. "Let me. Give me the right to make my own confession."

Something in this must connect with the attendant or then again maybe it is only the furious dancing and prancing, the frenzied caper of Blount's newly licensed

Messenger's hands, moving as if they were already entrapped in spleen. She looks, shrugs, presses a bell on the wall. Call buttons every three steps for emergencies. There are always emergencies in the Arena. "I can't take you there," she says, "that's not my assignment; we'll have to get someone else. Just wait now."

"Of course."

"Everything's specialized here."

"Me too," Blount says, "in my business."

"Your business. You're just out of the Institute, aren't you?"

"Who said that? Where'd you hear that?"

"*You* said it. Don't look at me like that." The gnome is agitated. His fingers twirl, winking and blinking he presses his head into the cool wall. All right. The moment is past. "You must be proud."

"Proud of what?"

"You're really someone now."

"Oh," Blount says, "I'm really someone. I'm really someone now. You'd better get that thing looked at lady; it's breaking down."

"Get what looked at?" the attendant says but her gesture implicates; she slams a hand across her cheekbones, fondles with coarse gestures until she has touched the spot. She has dreamed of the eruption of that wart. "What are you talking about?"

"That could spider-cancer," Blount says ungraciously, using his knowledge to terrify (this is immoral in certain cultures). "They do it all the time; remain inert for years and years and then *wham!* the filaments spread and you're done for in a week. It looks to me like it's coming into that stage; I'd get some advice on that soon."

"You—"

"No charge," Blount says, "no charge for what I've just told you," and strides jauntily down the corridor where another attendant, arms outstretched to take him Priestward greets him; this attendant younger and vaguely more attractive than the first but not significant. Never significant. She locks with Blount, this new attendant (the old one has been effectively removed from his consciousness forever).

"You want something?" she says. "What can I show you here?"

"You can take me to the Priest."

"How about a little something else?"

"Forget it. I'm neutered."

"You never know."

"I know."

"You could trust me," this attendant says somewhat petulantly, "you could give me a chance."

"I don't want any chances."

"How do you know you're neutered if you won't try?" She squeezes Blount's wrist; he can feel the pressure of her breasts rising horrid under a layer of silk, wicker of lips deadlier than knives against his ear. No jauntiness now; he has paid dearly for his moments, has Blount. "Come on," she says, "give it a try."

"I don't want to try anything."

"Off the tables, Messenger," she says. "Private rates. I always wanted to do a Messenger. Why can't I? I want to know what it's like to do it with someone that does what you do."

"Don't touch me!" Blount says. "Don't, don't you ever touch me!" shoving the attendant, feeling the resilience of her body now caving to waste under the pressure, all of the semen and women past their time, Downsiders often recruited for the Arena and devastated by it as no Institute could do. There are worse alternatives. "You fool!" he says. "You can't touch me; I'm poison, do you hear? I'm contaminated."

"Contaminated? Are you crazy?"

"All Messengers are crazy."

"No," she says to Blount, "no, they aren't; they just think they are, act that way, make the craziness," but

Blount has defeated her; she has lost and takes his hand wearily and with many shrugs. "It's a job, that's all," she says. "You've got to treat it that way."

"You'll never know."

"Oh, it isn't all that bad," she says, her features congealing toward an asexual slant, perfect for passing celibates and lunatics to the Priest. Showing that wonderful adaptability which characterizes the Arena which, no less than the Institute, has intricate policies and procedures. "There are worse things. You'll get used to it."

"I'll never get used to it," Blount says correctly, "ever. Take me to the Priest."

"In here," she says, "right in here," pointing through an alcove; all the time then they have been moving, cleverly in the proper direction, and now Blount can see the old machine, wires hanging in colors, planted awkwardly in a dusty corner. No one seems to have been in here for years. "It's right over there," the attendant says, "just go in and take it."

"That's all? Is it ready for use?"

"It's ready for use," the attendant says bitterly, "or it isn't ready for use but there it sits and I hope you're very happy with it just the two of you. No, don't say anything more. You can go to hell, you little freak," says the attendant with surprising vigor and goes away.

Satisfying. Blount finds this relaxing; the fact that the attendant hates him provides him with a feeling of human connection. He wanders into the alcove which is doorless, finds a screen huddled in a closet and places it in the opening of the room for privacy. These rooms canmay be used for copulation as well. But then everything in the Arena can be used for copulation, everything, which may be the basis of its success.

Blount looks at the Priest for a time. He wants to savor the moment; he has never been this close to one of the things. He has heard of them, read works of their great days in the low nineties when they were at the height of their popularity and the subject of popular songs (*Going to the Priest-is the least I could do for you-spill out my sins-between the grins I do feel blue-but the Priest will feast on you*), has familiarized himself with their greater and lesser weaknesses which resulted in their being discredited, for all intents and purposes, and relegated to the back rooms of the Arena. But he has never, at least until this moment, seen one and the image is of itself overpowering: here is an artifact in whom, at last, Blount can confide all of his problems, depositing his dreadful secrets one by one into its abscesses and obtaining in return the smooth change of absolution. His father was an artifact as well but has nothing on the Priest for dependability or mystery.

"The least I could do for you," Blount hums and seats himself before the machine, slivers of warmth passing between his little rear end and the chair as he lifts the headphones and by instinct (there have been no instructions but he is sure he knows what to do) activates the machine. Tapes whine; there is a deep thunk, the machine stirs.

"Clear," it says in a scratchy old voice. "This machine is clear and prepared for reception."

Formula. Blount remembers it all from the ancient and discredited texts; he speaks the words: "I have come to you for I have sinned."

"You have come to me to seek absolution for your sins," the machine says properly, the voice only faintly out of modulation. Blount is pleased; the machine sounds fine. Those had been good models in their day; he can hope then that this one has resources.

"I wish for you to hear me now for my sins are dark and most grievous." The texts redound; Blount knows the formula. He should; he has chanted it to himself on many nights.

"Confess, then, and be blessed. Confess and be blessed." A rasp; then an effeminate yowl on the *blessed*.

In the background, Blount hears the sounds of gearing. 1993 the plate says. Strange that he had not noticed this immediately. This must be one of the last models of the machine ever produced. Of course they had fallen well out of favor by then and quality control must have been lacking. Factories were being abandoned by the late 1980's; the workmen who tacked this together, Downsiders all, might have been sullen and incompetent. Well, Blount can hope. He will always hope. "Confess and be blessed," the machine says again. Blount detects impatience.

"I will confess. I am here to confess." Now he deviates from formula, trusting that the machinery has been primed; from now on he will strike into strange areas and hope that the gears, one last time, will collaborate. "I have just graduated," he says, speaking clearly and distinctly, "just today graduated from the Hulm Institute of Cancer Control where I completed training to become a Messenger." Hulm's Process did not go into commercial framework until the year 2000; will this Priest even know what the elf is talking about? "Messengers are reduced in size and go inside patients to remove small cancers by hand," he adds cautiously.

"A fine undertaking," says the Priest, confidently enough. "You surely take great pride in your accomplishment. Be not disappointed with yourself; discard all feelings of inadequacy." More ritual. Does the Priest understand? Of course, even if it does, it would still have to respond this way, Blount reminds himself. Bores in deeper.

"Hear me through," he says, "let me finish. The Hulm Institute of Cancer Control is a private and profit-making organization run under governmental sanction. It exploits the one stroke of genius which is its process and the terror of those who need it, both protected by irrevocable patent. It is utterly cynical and destructive, the Institute, that is to say. But then again, so are the patients." Callow youth! With what easy rage does Blount make his distinctions! with what clarity does he perceive the corruption of the universe. But do not hasten to blame him; he is doing the best he can. Furthermore, he is entitled to his rage; it is pure and shot through with fire. It will never be as pure again; Blount will learn to accept the world's corruption as soon as he discovers (with the help of Yancey, of course) his own.

"You have a right to react to your problems in the way you state. This is not doubted for a moment but you must learn that your rage is not productive. You can be shown a better course than this."

"Let me finish, let me finish," Blount says, quite excited now, overloading the machine (a mistake) with the floridity of his conversation rather than allowing it to control overloading through pauses. Foolish Blount! "The Institute is in the hands of greedy managers who, having controlled all of the rights to the Projector, its single innovation, now manipulate it for private gain. What should be a resource is a business."

"Youthful disillusion. It is common in persons of your generation and should not cause you undue concern. Now—"

"Shut up," Blount says. He is forgetful of the age and condition of the Priest; he has become possessed with his confession. Perhaps this is one of the reasons the process was discredited; Priests are really not able to deal with the material they evoke. Why did not Blount, knowing this through his researches, take the situation in measure and control himself? Why? Ah, there are no answers to this; there are no answers to anything. "You listen to me." the stricken youth says, "I want no platitudes. You are thirty years out of date, do you hear that? thirty years! but you're the best I can do, and I will be heard! I have learned and in the learning—"

"Tell me then," the Priest says, madly collaborating in its destruction. "Tell me all you wish," calling upon itself an overload. "Say whatever you wish and you will be heard. Confess and be blessed."

"Yes. Yes. I have readiness to confess and be blessed. I have learned the four causeways of cancer. I know its lesser and greater pathways, its colors and symbiosis. I have learned, now, the seventeen manual and forty-five automatic means of incision, I have learned of filaments, mitosis and the scatter of cells. I have seen demonstrations of the last inoperable stages, I have seen the deathbed syndrome as revealed by vault and ascension; under close supervision I ventured into the byways and alleys of the inoperable to learn the difference between the improbable and the hopeless. In my final assignment, not two weeks ago, I was permitted to solo on a clinic patient and I did not botch the job, saving him in the last moment, at the gut. I learned of the history and implications, volunteered for an elective course on the metaphysics of Messengering which was quite useless. I have bathed in the dark light of that Projector to feel myself shrink and die, have emerged quivering from the anus to feel the growing pain of restoration. All of these things and more I have done."

"Interesting; all of this sounds very interesting. You have had a rich and full life for one of your age, this is certain; you must take great pride in this."

"I take no pride."

"Detail your problem now."

"I said, I take no pride!"

"You must detail your problem. Speak loudly and enunciate with precision as you now explain your basis for requesting absolution."

"No chance. You will not let me speak."

"Confess. Confess and be blessed. No rest until you are blessed so confess. Know blessing and be released. Be released and do not be teased; say what you may and go on your way."

"Who needs confession in a whorehouse?"

"Do not stray. Do not personify but realify." The voice of the Priest has become somewhat querulous now but Blount in his agitation does not detect this nor other signs of the impending breakdown. "Why have you itemized?" the Priest asks, "when what you must cultivate is acceptance, the humility of the meek and the weak and the leakage of the wise."

Disordered Freudianism, peeking through the ruins of the Priest like flowers in gravelled Downside. Outmoded; outmoded even then, but the Priests were never given anything better. The time of the Priests ended when the Institute was born (and is there conversion between the two?) but the Freudianism staggers onward. Freudianism at the Arena!

"Impossible," Blount says, much disconcerted but still trying to make sense of the disaster (he does not know when to quit, you see; this is his basic problem or symptom), "you are not giving me a chance to speak my position."

"I am begging your pardon for this," the Priest says in the tiniest of voices. "What are you trying to say?"

And Blount pounds the walls of the cubicle in rage. Now he wishes that he had not alienated the attendant, because if she were there he could pound her instead and satisfying: satisfying it would be. He thinks of many things, beating his little fists on the wall: thinks how disgraceful it is that the Arena would have in a corner equipment of such a deteriorated condition while the rest of it, the rest of this arena: the sexual conversion pools, the fornicative quarters, the mind-darkeners, the hallucinative troughs, were all of the newest and most effective kind: it is not fair, Blount thinks, thinking for all he is worth that the oldest and boldest of impulses, that of confession, should be surely *insulted* in a manner like this. Oh no: there is no premium on confession in this culture, at least at the time of which Blount is thinking, confession belongs to the past or the future . . . but the contempt of the Arena, to have a Priest in condition such as this, is disgraceful. It only serves to illustrate, Blount's tiny mind cogitates, the eternal difference between purgation and escape as has been mapped out in so many of the great art works.

So he was justified. Justified in his thoughts, justified in his deeds. No less human than any of you, despite the pain of reduction, Blount performed the inevitable. That must be understood. There must be some respect for this man; any of you could have been in his deformed shoes if you had been there in his time.

"Let me finish," he says. "Please, let me explain." He will try it, then, for one last time. No reason to become inflamed, he tells himself, the peace that passeth all understanding instead must be cultivated. "I want to finish what I want to say."

"Finish, diminish. End, friend."

"I elucidate. I learned, then, all of the means of reduction to say nothing of the intricate and splendid history of the Hulm Projector itself, a most astonishing piece of equipment whose commercial application was put to work by Hulm himself, the only inventor-genius in human history who had a talent for marketing. I learned of Hulm himself, now ninety-two years old and as aptly vigorous as the day he had his stroke; I learned of the vision which drove him in the darkness toward a sense of accomplishment so terrific that it could only be sated by great amounts of money. Oh my God, the money in it!"

"You are sweating."

"What do you care?"

"You are sweating and evincing great rapidity of pulse. My sensors although damaged have picked up this information. Why do you react to data so cold with excitement? My sensors, runined by disuse as they are, remain alert. I know your condition."

"I have had enough of calm!" Blount says, pounding the machine. "I have been calm for four years; absorbing all that they have to teach me. Reasonable, calm men got me into this situation. Only rage can release me."

"But you cannot continue the confession at this emotional level. I must warn you, I am entering conditions of severe overload. Shortly I may circuit out and then where will you be? Calm, John. End, friend. Confess and be blessed. Diminish and be finished."

"How can you judge me like this?"

"Because you want to be judged. You have come here seeking my judgment; even a Priest does not have to be stupid. Some do not wish judgment but you do and therefore I must be all things to all men, *causus rex in excelsis*—"

"Everything to all of us, then," Blount said. "All along it was not concern, but a fiendish approach which would take in the lowest common denominator of feeling. They lied to us. All of them lied to us." Gritting his teeth, flapping his fingers, still trying to stride atop his mood, reckoning that on this, the most fundamental of all days, the Priest could only pose another challenge, slightly more hideous but hardly consequential. Nothing consequential, remember that: all of this is a joke in a vacuum. Nothing will matter. Blount dances in place, sways, kicks out, winks hideously at the machine, wills himself to control. Small man but a large heart, a greatness of the soul which cannot be ignored. Five foot two and is he blue, folks; think of him when you go on your way.

"I took the oath," he says. "I have been educated to all of the great and lesser evils into which the Messenger, however incorruptible, may fall. I have learned the ways of safety. I have learned the points of corpuscular disjunction or rupture and how to cunningly avoid them and today I received a drill and a headlamp, symbols of the station to which I have ascended. I received a lance, twice symbolic, an engraved diploma and the opportunity to buy a yearbook which will be mailed to me care of my new address or any relative who I may select at will. The cost of this, for my convenience, will be deducted from my first wages. Are you listening? Are you listening, you son of a bitch?"

"If you desire."

"I haven't even confessed yet!"

"If you desire."

"Listen then, listen now: I will make nineteen thousand dollars a year before taxation and this is only base scale. In half the period of my enlistment my wages will rise to fifty if I keep the lance straight and watch the compulsions. Isn't that remarkable? Fifty thousand dollars a year; the cost of one operation. I can get cancer, then, and with a year's work hire someone to dig it out. I have all of the advantages of which I would have been otherwise deprived in Downside. You've heard of Downside, haven't you? An excellent place, a remarkable address; nothing quite like it in the history of the world although, of course, you can say this about most places."

"If you wish."

"I had no future, the Institute nourished me."

"If you wish."

"I had no possibilities so the Institute made them manifest."

"Whatever you say."

"I had no hope and the Institute gave me a profession."

"Go and be blessed. Absolution has been granted."

"Absolution has not yet been asked. I have not even phrased my reason yet. All of the things I have said have been done for me, just as promised. They have saved me from Downside, they have sent me on my way. All of this is so and they have fulfilled all their commitments. I want you to tell me then—"

"Confess and be blessed."

"Tell me why I hate them. Why do I hate them so?"

Lights waver on the Priest in threads of green. "Pardon me," it says. There is a hum, pause; Blount has a vague feeling of transcendentalism as matters shift to another level. "I am now on automatic," the Priest says in a new voice. "What has happened is that there has been an an overload in the circuitry. I warned you. You were warned. It is only a slight problem which technicians will swiftly correct. Attendants will come. Be patient and of good cheer; I have signaled for the restoration."

"Why do I hate them so?"

"Restoration will arrive."

"I hate them; I hate them!" Blount says, chanting irrythmically, mumbling and grumbling away, heedless of the warning of the stricken machine. The walls of the room seem to be closing in on him; in a hot, sweaty little box Blount twitches and jumps. "I hate them, hate them!" he says again. "If only I knew the answer to this, if only I could explain my hatred, I would be free. Everything else now I have come to believe but not that. You must help me. I tell you: you must help me!"

"My circuitry is now overloaded," the Priest confesses. "Please be patient with me. There is some small problem in the mechanics;" it confides, "an attendant will come and service, this will be corrected. There are numerous attendants waiting upon my every need," it remarks, "and if you will be patient I will be returned to full efficacy. Very little time will elapse," it promises, "and then I will be truly functional again."

"Oh, no, you don't do this to me you son of a bitch!" the crazed Blount says, pounding metal, admitting his shame. "You can't get off that easily. Listen to me you bastard and tell. I want the truth; I have been told to believe in it and I do, I accept those lessons, now at last I must learn—"

"Please desist in further conversations," the Priest murmurs, "for I now risk serious damage. If you will wait and be patient—"

"Where are the attendants?"

"They are coming."

"There are no attendants. No one cares anymore. You're thirty years old and slipping downhill; no one believes in you any more. They couldn't service you if they wanted. You're dead, dead!"

"Never—"

"I made my statement and I want to confess. I want to confess! This is my right; this is your role and here is the confession I will give to you." Blount at last is getting to the point. Now and then he has had difficulties in summary but at last it seems he will approach the issue. "Here is my confession," the little guy says. "I want to kill! Not to cure, but to kill!"

"Oh," the Priest says noncommittally. "*Oh.* I am on overload; my circuitry—"

"All of my life I was maimed, blasted, burned, sullied and profits were turned off these deprivations; now they have taken me from Downside and told me of a future—but I do not want a future. I do not want the Hulm Projector nor to absorb its dreadful lessons. I do not want to clamber inside the rich and terminal like a bug to yank out their cancer. This is what I realized during the ceremony. As I took that oath I breathed hatred; it came to me in that terrible completion that I hate all of it. I will not go through this anymore. I refuse. I repudiate. I wish absolution."

"But I am not functional. My circuitry overloaded is. Patience and mendacity lying quietly side by side, signaling oh so quietly two by two in the night and looking for an attendant soon will pass and then well again all must speak for the now of the bough and then well, sell, hell again for speaking but it be hard and dark and strange so watch the confessions—"

"I have no interest in diminution," Blount points out fervidly. Communication with the Priest seems to have arrived at a different level but who is not to say, considering this, that contact is not being made at a level even more profound? "I am terrified of being five-eightieths of an inch tall. The soul cannot be contained in corridors so limited nor can the intellect; I will become impacted upon myself and disappear. What if they have lied to us? What if the Projector proves someday to be irreversible after all and I remain five-eightieths of an inch? What jar would they put me in? I hate the forty-five ways. I hate the pathways. Let me tell you this," Blount says, pounding on the Priest, little sparks flying from the exposed coils as he does so, "I want out of this. Because if I do not get it, I am going to kill."

"Is coming now an attendant," the machine advises, "attendant to sing the congealing blood, opening the panels and wiring night the attendant will render repairs—"

"Kill!" Blount says. "I want to kill! Do you understand me? Do you finally, finally understand that?" He rises to his full height, five feet one and full of fun, possessed of liquor backing through him now, heaving upwards and outwards, inflating him to sixty-one inches of power and rage, and hurls himself against the metal, battering tiny hands against the steel. His delicate little feet pound on the damnable iron and at this moment Blount must abandon some last reserve of control because, by dint of the most earnest application, he begins to work upon the Priest fervently, spinning broken controls, wrenching at the dials like nipples, making sounds that might be taken for the moans of lust if there were not so much loss in it.

"Please," the Priest squeaks, final self-preservative tendencies coming into play. "You cannot—"

"You too!" Blount screams. "You don't want to listen! No one wants to listen to me; no one wants to hear, you're not even *there* you damnable machine, godammit!" The air is filled with metal, flying parts, coils and strips of wire and at the center of this metal is Blount, throwing it like a juggler but no fielding on the rebound, the metal falling instead in a series of crashes *ting!* to the floor, Blount shouting, the machine gasping, the walls contracting, the machine managing to mutter on even *in extremis,* "confess and be blessed . . . conblessed and befess," and in Blount's extremity he thinks that the machine might be *mocking him* indignant elf that he is so he continues his passionate work upon the coils until the unfortunate Priest is literally disassembled on the floor.

"All you ever wanted was to use me," Blount says rather confusedly; grant him mercy, however, this man does not quite know what he is saying (and for that matter never did) and may be pardoned, then, his small slips of reasoning. "Rigged, manipulated, all of it!" he says enthusiastically, ranting on and on until it occurs to him in a bound that the machine is completely demolished and, therefore, that he may not even call upon a witness for his ravings. Finally: finally then, Blount is quiet. Through small shifts and twitches he moves into a neutral zone of activity. He folds himself upon himself on the floor and for a while he says nothing.

Oh Blount! Blount! try conceiving some feeling for him, conjure mercy from conception; not all of this was his fault, he was drunk. So drunk that as he lies mumbling and battered on the floor he finds himself wishing that his hands were stone: stone so that he could have smashed the damned Priest, smashed this attendant of corruption so that it could bear witness no longer, and caving in upon himself, newly confirmed and unfortunate Messenger upon the floor, Blount does not hear that whore, the attendant who comes into the room at last to see what has happened. Summoned not by his screams but only the expiration of the time she nevertheless understands the situation fully and without the need for explanation; plunges to him at last then and encircles him in her arms. An embrace fierce and warm as death consumes the tired Blount then as barely aware of it he mutters in his place upon the floor. The attendant grips him more tightly, shifts her breast up and down the complacent panels of his back, sighs and strokes his hair.

"Please now," she says to Blount, not releasing her hold, "please, don't feel, don't scream, it isn't as bad as you have to make it; all that you have to do is to live. Live and live with it," nuzzling Blount then with lips like iron, that last sweet memento of the Arena. "We could have done something," the attendant says, "we could have become something," and it must be this which flips the hapless Blount all the way over the line because it is at that moment—and not until its expiration, his reserves have been strong; he has held on—that Blount at last faints, tumbling into the attendant and over her, falling and falling into the harsh matrix of the Arena as time closes over.

7

"Please," she had said to Blount in the hall, "I want you to kill him. He's got to die." And then at the expression in Blount's eyes, a certain steely determination in his face which she must have taken for disapproval instead of the mask or terror which it truly was, had backed off from him into the wall, her fine, high buttocks arched there, standing in place, shuffling invisible objects from one hand to the other. "All right," she said, "forget that I mentioned it." But Blount closed in upon her, one hand still raised for astonishment's sake, trying to establish communion and then she caved in like water, found a small open place in the area between them and ran. "I'll deny it," she said, "I'll deny it!" and then was gone before Blount had a chance to tell her—

—before Blount had a chance to tell her that it was not disapproval but only astonishment, that he has been misread and never another chance to talk to her because she has pelted down the halls, launched herself into a stairwell, nurses and attendants standing there, looking with bemusement at this fleeing relative, their glances at last bouncing from the stairwell to Blount himself who, you can be sure, stood there with a great deal of puzzlement shrouding his attractive features, showing his palms in an expression of vulnerability and dismay. What has Blount done? those glances say, what has the lunatic done to this young girl? the notoriety of Messengers already being well-established of course and their well-known reputation for instability augmented by this pretty flight, the stairwell door still banging in reminiscence, Susan Forks now racing through the grounds of the Institute, possibly bearing news of Blount's unspeakable assault upon her.

He waits then for the nurses and attendants to close in upon him, Blount does. He waits for trays to be put down, needles to be pushed aside, jackets to be unbuttoned and slowly, slowly the hospital personnel will advance. *You assaulted a patient's visitor,* an imposing intern will say. *We always knew Messengers were insane but this is impossible* the young blonde nurse will point out. *We're going to call the Director and have you recommitted to Downside* they will all aver. But they do not advance. They stay in place.

They stay in place and it occurs to Blount in small waves and throbbings of energy that they are not going to; that they have been convinced, for whatever obscure reasons, to keep their distance. They will not be moved. They will not be moved because their knowledge of Messengers has already convinced them that the entanglements are beyond their doing. Nothing happens, then. Nothing happens at all.

Blount stays where he is for a while, absorbing the First Great Lesson of the Yancey Case—that given the options he has sacrificed, there is now nothing he cannot get away with if he does it carefully, carefully—and then with a shrug and a little nod at his co-workers on the eighteenth floor, turns from them with posture solemn and sprightly and adjusts himself to go back to the room to perform further gross monitoring tests upon the supine but highly consequential form of Yancey.

8

Blount, on the screen, is leaning over Yancey's body on the bed, his hindquarters and elbows at least momentarily blocking the angle of the camera into his patient but now, as that camera barrels straight in, Blount, with some reluctance, turns away from his ministrations and we can see Yancey, open to the camera under the bedsheets, an old, old man with eye-shaped mouth, pursed into a blind O at the ceiling, his limbs flapping wearily as Blount slaps and rolls them to preserve muscle tone. It is the second day post-operative; Yancey is in contact most of the time, the sedative block functioning from the lumbar rather than the cerebrum-region, meaning that he has been restored to the full contours of his consciousness if not yet motility.

"Dirty sons of bitches!" Yancey says, a characteristic phrase of his as Blount has already discovered. "They're all out to get you, every step of the way. Go a little easier on that son, you want to knot me up you corrupt little thief? That's more like it now. Ah. *Ah.*" Sexual moans and groans overtake Yancey, he succumbs to Blount's careful attempts to restore circulative facilities to the lower legs.

Blount has not yet taken more definite action. The decision to kill, once accomplished, has never been retracted in Blount's experience and he knows that he will not retract it this time either but the methodology still evades him and he feels wickers of hesitance. Yancey must die; there is no doubt about it, but if his death is not accomplished in a certain way and from a certain perspective, it will be a failure. Blount, therefore, must bide his time. Yancey will be in the Institute for four days more; plenty of time to accomplish it and meanwhile he can gather strength. The elf's attempts to elicit information from the granddaughter have failed: all right then, let it be. Blount's life has been filled with failure, one more setback at this stage hardly matters. He will have to attack the source itself.

Yancey. He will learn everything he has to know from Yancey himself then; Blount does not doubt his facility or the willingness of the old man to talk. Sneaking around the biographic edges will accomplish nothing and was a doomed gesture from the beginning; go directly to the source then and allow the old man to reveal himself. The life of Yancey will be deduced by what can be reconstituted within this bed in a matter of hours; allow one kicker as well to lend spice to the investment . . . if Yancey can explain himself in a way which Blount will find justifiable, Blount will not kill him. The Messenger is not an unreasonable man; within him palpitates a heart as wise and true as that in the best of you and if Yancey can prove why he deserves not to be murdered, well, then, Blount will not murder him. In the meantime, it is necessary to circle ever more dimly into the center of the mystery.

"Lousy bitch!" Yancey says as Blount swabs him unlovingly with a sterile cloth, trying to induce the renewed circulation now to flow upwards and through the higher centers of the body. "Lousy, dirty bitch, that's all she is!" Blount deduces that the old man must be talking about Susan Forks. "Doesn't give a good goddamn about nothing," Yancey murmurs as the whisk of cloth continues unabated, "but that's all right; she's going to get hers too. They all get theirs sooner or later, even old Yancey. Thought I was done for son. Go a little easier on me you bastard, you're scraping the skin."

Blount urges himself to go a little easier, hoping that

further evidences and materials on Susan Forks will come to him. If she can be explained then everything will fall into place, or so the Messenger has decided. Do not think that his reasoning is without profundity or point; it was he who only hours ago bounced and jounced within the hidden partitions of old Yancey; if this does not give a man a certain sense of perspective, nothing will. Blount could close his eyes and see Yancey's gut as it hung so luminescent before him not two days ago if he tried; this is a connection which cannot be minimized. Who of you could make that statement about any of your friends, lovers or acquaintances?

"What's wrong with her," Blount says oh so quietly, in the teeny-tiniest of Messenger's voices as he eases more lukewarm water upon Yancey and works it into the pores. "Why do you say that she has to get hers?"

"Is it any of your business son?" Yancey says, his old eyes blinking. He opens and closes his eyes repeatedly like a heartbeat, raising his hands to the ceiling. "I know what's going on here," he says. "They can't fool me."

"What's going on here?" the ever-patient Blount says: swabbing, swabbing. Yancey accepts these ministrations with sighs and small bubbling sounds of contentment; he has accepted Blount, it would seem, on a higher and deeper level. "You can talk to me if you want," Blount adds soothingly, completing his tasks for the moment and dropping the rag back into a shallow basin, then taking a towel to rub Yancey dry. The skin bunches under the towel, feels to Blount's fingers as if it might dislocate and come off in his hands but it is amazing, simply amazing, how neutrally one can approach a disgusting task if one has cultivated simple resignation. "You know you want to talk," Blount says with what he takes to be shrewdness, "so just go ahead and tell me."

"I won't tell you anything son," the old man says, closing his eyes now with a portion of finality. "Not a word; you're always sneaking and peeking around, all of you trying to find out secrets; my secrets are my business. I've paid my money and that's all that matters. The dirty bitch!" Yancey says, a smile curving up and around his face. "I'll take care of her, I really will; she'll regret this." and then, quite surprisingly, he sleeps. The transition to somnolence is instant; one moment the old man is talking, the next he is not, his breath pouring even and regularly from his mouth. No coma, no stroke. Blount checks the gross signs and finds to his relief that everything is in order. He completes his tasks and puts the towel into a disposable bag, then somewhat clumsily stands looking at Yancey for a while.

No contact. Blount expects something enormous to happen; Yancey will begin to talk in his sleep of the true reasons for the hatred of his granddaughter, Yancey will leap from the bed screaming that Blount is a murderer, that he is going to murder him, Yancey will enter a physical crisis so acute that nothing whatsoever will occur to Blount for the next few hours other than the need to save the old man for the murder. But nothing. Nothing of it. The scene wavers, drifts into a series of pastel shades, flowers and music cut in from the background. Still-life: devoted Messenger and his recovering patient, alone together in their room. Blount cannot bear it. He cannot bear the sentimentality of it. None of his life has conditioned him for feeling and this is not the proper place to begin, the proper object for emotion. He turns. He lunges toward the door. (He has done all of this before.) He flees the room, although he is not sure of his destination.

In the hallway is Susan Forks. She must have been standing there, waiting to get him, or so Blount thinks in his agitation. She lays determined fingers upon his sleeve, lays her determined body against his, horrid little reactions go through Blount's tiny frame as she gathers him in.

"I can't put it off anymore," this woman now says to

him, appearing massive in Blount's distorted perspective, not twenty-three but ageless, a spiritless force of gathering, "You'll misunderstand everything. We are going to talk," Susan Forks says, "we are going to talk about everything now." She seizes the hapless Blount by an arm. "I've straightened this out in my own mind and I know we've got to talk," she says. She urges Blount into the corridor. He moves at increasing speed. They pass the nurses' station in acceleration. They approach the elevator. "Yes, I'm going to tell you everything," Susan Forks says and from a great distance the doors of an elevator open and close upon the pair like the branches of a tree containing birds and they disappear from view.

9

Blount constructs a dark, spiralling fantasy of what might occur between him and Yancey's granddaughter granted circumstances. In this fantasy Susan Forks, highly influential with the administration of the Institute, has arranged for Blount to be relieved of his commitments to the patient for several hours and now she has taken him to the hotel room near the Institute which she has rented for the duration of the treatment. The room is cluttered and filled not only with the personal possessions of Susan but with memorabilia of Yancey which she has brought in at the old man's imperious demand: ancient Bibles and stock certificates in the Yancey trunk compete for space with bottles of whiskey and ancient correspondences in which, forty years before, people pleaded with Yancey for mercy.

"Forget this," Susan says in the dream to Blount, waving a dismissive hand at the room, the windows, the possessions. In a sweeping gesture she divests herself of all her clothing, stands before Blount naked and insistent, Yancey's only granddaughter's little breasts prodding up and outward at him. "Come here," Blount dreams she says to him, "I want you now, I want you desperately. Messengers excite me, thinking that you went right down into grandfather's bowels and poked around in there, that's terribly exciting, don't you think? Getting inside a person's body like that. Come on, get inside my body," she says rather flatly and then falls upon the bed, collapsing as if from the great height, spreading her legs then with a sigh to invite Blount's entrance.

Still dressed, the little fellow stands before her in a state of middle confusion. He tries to imagine the cameras, the omnipresent cameras of his life clearing a path of vision from the ceiling, rumbling and grumbling along as they record this new disastrous incident but the presence of the cameras yields him none of the usual comforts (Blount by believing that his life is under constant observation for a paying audience, has managed to make himself feel important, although desperate. Instead he feels them tearing, ripping, opening up huge gashes on his life and sensibility.

"Don't you want me?" Susan says, arching her back off the bed and demonstrating to Blount her breasts. "What's wrong with you? I can't be the first girl that was excited by a Messenger."

"You don't understand," Blount dreams he says, peeping and piping. "I've never, I mean I never did this; I mean I tried to say—" and he stumbles into incoherence watching her. This information seems to affect Susan as little as anything he has said, her gestures becoming only more insistent.

"Come on," she says, "take me now; don't you want to learn about my grandfather? You will—after you fuck me."

Blount, elfin, grave, dreams that he takes off his clothing finally, tearing off his robes and dropping them to the floor with a clank from all the equipment contained therein; then slowly, carefully moves upon the girl. As he does so her eyes at last close, her breathing flattens, she stops speaking and opening her mouth slightly to moisten her lips with tongue, tosses back her head to show the open spaces of her neck and throat, extending her arms then to gather Blount in, already locked, solitary, into the motions of generation. Blount feels the heat coming from her, kneels on the bed, poises himself over her and then, in this dream, like a man trapped in a dream, slowly guides himself over and against her, trying to force tumescence by a series of quick slashing motions below, urging life to come into his teeny-tiny flapping organ that has been erect, so far as he knows, only at moments when not observed.

"Ah!" the girl says, "oh!" and "my God," words and sounds which Blount has never heard before but which do not surprise him since he knows from his clinical background how they are supposed to act, then, fumbling, she seizes and twirls his little organ and tries to make insertion. Her eyes come open.

"What's wrong?" she says. "What the hell is wrong with you?"

Her breasts tremble, her very nipples darken with disapproval.

"No one does this to me," she says. Clearly she is very angry; the contours of the fantasy itself take a different shape, become hard-edged and jagged, knifing their way like splinters into Blount's consciousness but he cannot, no matter how he tries, disentangle. He is locked in.

"Are you crazy?" she says as if Blount's little prick were a mind that had been unsettled, but her body is the cheat now because for all of the words she has said her body is still an invitation, curled into a question mark on the bed and Blount, held by her, is unable to establish distance. Finally he caves against her, feels her breasts winging into his hands, feels a flare opening in the vicinity of his bowels which might be confused with hope and for a moment, as he batters against her, thinks that indeed he might be functioning, something is growing there, something is happening and with his eyes closed, squeezing images against the retinas in the blankness Blount is able to convince himself that he may be on the verge of a major breakthrough . . . but as his struggles increase, as the girl's body turns cold underneath him he realizes in this dream that nothing is happening. He is softer than ever before, his wee prick seemingly almost vanished into the folds of his crotch as he takes a little peek. Poor, helpless Blount! What is to be said about him?

What indeed? In the dream he rolls from Susan, investigates little cracks and openings in the ceiling, plaster caving, chalky fragments whisking like silt upon the two of them, engraving little ashen pictures over their bodies.

"Do you see now?" he says at last in the dullest, flattest voice, speaking distinctly so that the microphones will be able to pick this up. (The image of being taped for posterity is back and holding more strongly than ever; he imagines the audience poised at knife-edge for this most thunderous of all revelations), "I can't do a thing. I tried and it doesn't work. Now tell me about your grandfather. I kept my part of the bargain; you keep yours."

A terrible thing to say but Blount has never cultivated the amenities; amenities are hardly for Messengers who must creep, day by day, through a portion of life which holds no secrets whatsoever. But it sounds harsh to him, must sound harsher to the girl for she turns from him, slamming her little jutting buttocks against his helpless crotch, her body like iron, tense with revulsion now and Blount must detach himself from her to avoid being burned by the cold which comes from those buttocks.

"Listen," he says gently in this dream, touching the girl on the shoulder and trying to draw her attention, speaking hopelessly against the flat panels of her back, trying now as he never has before (pity this man!) to tell the absolute truth, "listen, you don't understand. The Projector neuters us. The process, exposing ourselves to the Projector, the contraction, destroys the glands you're looking for. We can't function," Blount says. At last his small mystery is revealed but how can it be a mystery? He thought that everyone knew this about the Messengers; even he did years ago. "It's nobody's fault, it's just the Projector," he says. "If you're going to be a Messenger then you're going to lose the ability to function sexually, that's understood from the beginning. They don't cheat us or mislead us at all; everyone knows this. Didn't you know it?"

Still she says nothing. Her body does not move, she lies in an uneven heap on the bed, breathing quietly. What is she thinking? Does it matter? Does anyone care? Yes, Blount finds himself thinking; yes he does care; he wants to know what she is thinking and this for him is the simplest mystery of all for he has never cared until this moment for anyone's opinion of him; he lived only in terms of his own valuations.

"You see," he says, "the kind of man who would become a Messenger to start wouldn't care too much about losing that part of himself. It's a price he's willing to pay. I never had any feeling," he says, "never had any feeling at all; maybe it was late adolescence, maybe it was my father, maybe it was just Downside, but that part of me was always dead so I didn't even have to calculate a decision. Some of us do. Some of them can't make the transition; when they learn what the Projector is doing to them they go a little bit insane. They know all the facts beforehand but some are stupid and think that it won't happen to them and it's only when they find it in the evidence of their own bodies that the craziness starts. There are actually people in this world, even people who come from Downside, who cannot understand something until it's shown to them. But I knew it," Blount says, "I knew that I was going to lose it. But how can you lose something you never had? I didn't care. I tried," he says, "I tried to tell you but you wouldn't listen. No one listens, ever. No one wants to hear what we have to say; even the people we go inside like your grandfather don't want to admit that we exist. It's tragic but that's the way it is. I'm sorry," he says finally. He has never, as far as he knows, said this to anyone before. "Really sorry."

His confession finished he awkwardly sits tailor-fashion on the bed, looking down at his microscopic genitals which gaze at him, the one blind eye of his penis, with an expression solemn and ungiving, and then gets off the bed. It is all over, at least in this dream. He will leave.

The girl will say nothing. Why will she say nothing? Blount casts earnest glances back at the bed as he dresses, harumphs to himself, contrives a despairing sob or two hoping for the response of inquiry but there is only silence. This is definitely unfair of her; the least that she could do is speak. What is wrong with her? Why will she say nothing? Dressed at last, feeling somewhat more in command of himself from within the hollow of his robes, Blount returns to the bedside, puts a hand on the girl's shoulder. She is quiet. Breath does not move under her skin. Has she died then? This would be Blount's luck. Even in fantasies; he will give himself only the worst of outcomes.

He digs his fingers into her flesh, turns her toward him. She rolls easily, quickly upon her back. Blount gazes down upon her. She is not dead. She is not, in fact, even Susan Forks. She seems to have become during this interval, as a matter of fact, someone else. He thinks he recognizes her but he cannot be sure. Then it all comes to him in a rush. Of course. She has become the whore-attendant of the Arena who took him to the Priest. How long has he been addressing her, thinking that she is the gentle granddaughter of Yancey?

"Talk to me, you bitch!" he says. "What are you doing here? What do you want of me?" and she gives him what seems to be in sleep the gentlest and most terrible of smiles, a madonna-smile full of mystery and loathing, licking her lips again in the gesture that was Susan's.

"I knew," she says quietly. "I knew that we could get you to open up if we only took the right approach. You see? you would have confessed all the time if we could only find the handle to it," and this is definitely too much for Blount; too much for even his rich and subtle intelligence to contain in fantasy; it all caves in around him and like a man drowning, moving frantically through underwater to some hint of oxygen he rises and rises, gasping and groaning with the overload of it, coming all the way to the surface and at the surface is the very reasonable and composed Susan Forks looking at him across a table as bare and gleaming as an operating area and saying, "What's wrong with you? You look terrible. Is there something about my grandfather that you haven't told me yet?"

10

Three scant days before his graduation from the Institute, Blount had occasion to visit his father who was in a terminal disease ward at the Metropolitan Unit, quickly disintegrating with cancer. The enlistment bonus had come in handy; had pushed the senior Blount through four major new systems and several minor; but all things must come to an end, even money, and the last six months had been very difficult for the courageous old man who had solved his final problems of penury, at least, by contracting the dread disease and thus obtaining free room and board at the only unit actually operating within the confines of Downside.

"Goddamn it, I'm glad to see you, son," the considerably weakened Blount senior said as Leslie sidled to his bedside, wearing a mask and gown for protection, twisting his little fingers into knots so that there would be as little contact on any level with his father. (Years in the Institute had taught Leslie the value of superstition; he does believe now that cancer can be passed on via manual contact.) "But you sure took your time getting here."

"Sorry about that," Leslie said, backing away from his father and occupying a neutral zone somewhat westerly of the bed, ignoring meanwhile the stares and glares of surrounding patients, all of them devastated old men similar in appearance to Blount senior although lacking, perhaps, that mad gleam in senior's eyes which had always characterized him. "Been very busy with the studies you know and besides I only got your note a few days past."

"Sure son, sure," Blount senior said, winking and blinking, making gestures toward his son. "This is my boy," Blount senior said to the surrounding beds. "He's come to save me." Grumbling and approvals throughout the room. "Glad you finally got here, son," Blount said. "I was getting pretty worried there for a while but I knew you'd come through. Knew that you wouldn't be looking me up while you were in the Institute because of the studying and all and besides I wanted you out of Downside but when things came to sevens, I knew I could count on you. Always knew it."

He struggled to his elbows, fixed Blount with a bright, stuporous, birdlike wink. "Is it all arranged?" he said. "When am I going to get out of here? Or are you going to do the operation from here after all? That's all right; anything you say. How soon do you think you can get in there son; I'm hurting bad. I know what I've got."

"I'm afraid," Blount said delicately, a casual flip of his fingers (oh, he had cultivated some manners within the Institute although not too damned many), "I'm afraid I don't know what you're talking about."

"Of course you know what I'm talking about son; here you are, traveled five hundred miles to see your old man in this condition and I always knew that you would be that kind of son. Knew that if it came right down to the tough going you'd be at the bedside. Oh, I didn't know if I should call on you son; had my doubts right until the last moment but knew too that you wouldn't fail me and here you are. Here you are. Tell me this, son," Blount senior said, urging himself from the bedclothes and forcing himself up on a forearm to whisper close to Blount's ear, "are you going to do the work yourself or is it better if an outsider does it? Know the truth; you'd feel a little uncomfortable moving around your old man's true gut now, wouldn't you? But I trust you son and if that's the way it has to be, then that's the way. The important thing is that you do it quick, boy," Blount senior said, subsiding on the bedclothes with a croak, "because the fact is that I'm failing fast and that's the truth. Every day a little bit more of me gets taken out. I never thought it would be like this. I knew it could eat you away piece by piece but I wasn't ready for the pieces of the brain they were taking out. Oh my lad," the old man said and with a trembling, hasty grip seized Blount's forearm and squeezed it, "I am so terribly glad to see you because I am failing fast. You'd best do the deed now while there's part of the old man still left to play."

"You don't understand," Blount said. He had traveled five hundred miles to see his father, this much was true —and in order to understand this scene you must comprehend the background; Blount suffers from an old compulsion to divulge enormous and extraneous amounts of information—and had battled his way to the old man's bedside with an admixture of grief and curiosity, looking at the old bugger, held in place at last, however, and for once without a framework of options, the grief had faded to a kind of clinical detachment and then backed off even further than that; Blount found himself considering his now wasted father, fifty years old, as he had been trained to look at many a patient in the Institute, preparatory to the initial experimentation.

"You don't understand any of it I'm afraid. I haven't come here to help you. I can't help you."

"Haven't come here to help me?" senior said. "Of course you have, why else would you be here? Look at me son," he said, drawing the bedclothes away and exposing himself in hospital gown, the thin folds both revealing and concealing everything of his father that needed to be known. "You've *got* to help me son. What you been studying there for four years now except how to help cases like me? And anyway, the families of Messengers are entitled to free treatment. I know that just as well as you do. You can look it up; it's all in print, just like the bonus clause."

"But you don't understand," Blount said, smooth, compassionate, condescending at last having become, if only for the moment, the man that he always wanted to be, noting that the other patients, attuned to the drift of the conversation were watching him with that unusual acuteness and attention which he had hitherto reserved to the moving picture productions of his mind, "there's nothing that can be done for cases like yours. Messengers can't go in there and excise large tumors; they can only get them in the early stages or go in and clean out the fibers after gross surgery. Neither applies in your case. You're a very sick man. You've got an intestinal cancer which has tossed subsidiary tendrils all the way through the digestive tract; part of the network has already reached the esophagus. I've read the charts and I know." Oh how Blount relished this technical language! How it came from him with the ease of a yielding sigh! And how the surrounding old men in the ward took in every word of it; it was enough to make Blount feel that all of his time in the Institute had not, after all, quite been misspent. "It's quite hopeless," Blount said, taking the bedclothes and bringing them neatly up to the chin of his stricken father, tucking them around the old man's features tightly in the way that a good embalmer might get a subject ready before commencing his tasks. "If you're looking for any help from me I'm afraid that you've made a terrible mistake. You can't be helped."

"Can't be helped?" the old man said. "What do you mean I can't be helped?" He turned, gesticulated to the room, called the waning attention of the old men back into focus again. "I've got to be helped! You wouldn't have come otherwise. Stop lying to me, Leslie. Get me prepped for the operation and get this damned stuff out. You wouldn't cheat an old man, would you?"

"Yes, I would."

"Stop it, Leslie!"

"Of course I would," Blount said, his resolve for calm reaking slightly. "Why do you think I came all this disance to see you? To help you? The hell I did; it meant hat I could get out of the Institute for a day while I ooked you over. Besides I wanted to see you—I wanted o make sure that you were really dying. You are really ying."

"No I'm not!"

"Of course you are," Blount said. "You're dying all the ime. You won't last more than a couple of weeks, less if hey take you off the sedatives; but they're probably sing you for observation and experimentation like most f the cases down here so they'll keep you going for a while and then pull you off suddenly. You can count on t least another three weeks, maybe a month."

"Leslie, you've got to help me!" Blount senior said. He icked the sheets feebly, attempted to rise again, thought etter of it, lay back and seemed to blend with the bedheets. Twenty-five years of the maiden colt and gelding ystem seemed then to open a tap which flooded resignaon into his face. "You mean it," he said after a pause. You really do mean it. You're not going to do anything t all to help me."

"Of course not," Leslie said. "In the first place you're uite beyond help and in the second I wouldn't do anyhing even if I could. Aid to the families of Messengers is ptional, do you know that? You'd need the permission f the Messenger and I've already denied that permison."

"Stop talking to me, son."

"I wouldn't give my permission if it meant my life," lount says, not entirely truthfully. "If my life was on e line for denying the operation to you I wouldn't have ny part of it; that's how much I want to see you dead! I came here five hundred miles just to make sure that i was real, that the messages weren't false. I wanted t look on you and see the end coming."

"Recrimination, Leslie!" his father said. "This terribl recrimination will get you nowhere. Believe me son, have seen all the devices of the haters in my time and tell you they all come to nothing." Then: "All right," h said, lying down and pulling the covers up to his jawlin "You've seen what you wanted to see; now you may go

"That's right," Blount said, only a little shakily, "an that's what I'm going to do now. I'm going to go."

"It won't do you any good, son."

"Nothing does me any good."

"All of these people around me will remember this— they won't remember what I was, Leslie; they'll remem ber you. They'll remember the kind of son I have an that he came five hundred miles to see his old man die.

"But they'll all be dead too, so it doesn't matter. Ther isn't a memory in this ward which will last more tha two months."

"Sad, Leslie. I would have hoped that the opportun ties you were given, the chances that you had, woul make something different of you. But I was wrong. I wa wrong about everything. Well, there's no cure for this, Blount senior said, "more than there's a cure for anythin else, so I'll just have to live with it. Goodbye, Leslie."

"Goodbye," Blount said. The glances of the old me were penetrating upon him, giving Blount a strange feel ing of warmth as he made his way from the bed and h had the vague feeling that somehow he had misunder stood the point of the meeting. He had come to his fa ther with one set of purposes in mind—to utterl humiliate and destroy the old man, avenge himself upo his father at last—and found himself leaving in anothe mood. No remedy for it. No remedy for anything in thi strange and distorted relationship which had neverthe less given Blount so much feeling over the years, mor feeling than he would ever know again. "Goodbye, goodbye."

"I never wanted to take the bonus from you, you know. It was just that I wanted to take the money in your interest because you never would have been able to hold onto it. It's all safe," Blount's father said with an odd cackle, "every cent of it. You'll find it in the will, when they open the boxes."

"You're crazy. You're lying."

"No I'm not. Besides, what do you care, Leslie? You've made your position already."

"You'd never be here. You'd never be in Downside. You would have used that money to get out of this if you had any of it left at all. It went on the horses."

"No it didn't," Blount senior said. To Leslie's tortured vision it seemed as if the old man stuck his tongue out deliberately before squirreling underneath the covers. "All of it was saved for you. I deposited it in your interest, Leslie, and it's still growing, growing, while your old man dies a Downsider."

And then Blount senior refused to say anything more. Blount came to the bedside, compelled at last to listen to his old man, poking and prying at the bedclothes to start the conversation again but spitefully the old man worked himself in deeper, would say nothing. His wardmates also pulled covers over their heads, lay there inert; only the sounds of tubing and intravenous dripping from the beds of some gave indication that there was life still left in the ward.

"You can't do this to me!" Blount shrieked over the adamant form of his father. "You can't get away with something like this." But the damned old man would say nothing, the others would say nothing, no one would say anything at all and at last Blount had to leave, somewhat assisted by attendants who had heard disturbances in the ward and had felt it best to eject the young Messenger.

"Don't worry about anything," one of the attendants

said, guiding Blount through a door, "but on the other hand, you'd better never come back here again."

And then there was Blount, outside the swinging doors, in the elevator alcove and alone, rising within him a sense of betrayal so large and astonished that he knew he might be years in finally coming to terms with it. At length the elevator came and took him away, that is to say that the elevator took him from this one level and deposited him at another level, but in an essential sense it did not take Blount away from that ward and has not yet, judging at least from his activities and bearing over recent days.

He is still in the ward, he is still leaning over the bedside of his father. Dead eight months ago of the cancer that killed him like a grenade in the stomach, Blount senior is yet alive, his eyes dancing with knowledge and humor as he looks upon his son from his vantage point against the pillows.

"You'll never learn," he says to his son against the whining and hiss of the tubes, the scurrying in the halls, "never, never learn anything at all; see, the money is all intact, I didn't take a penny of it, saved it all for you," and Blount arched over that bed has no reply whatsoever remembering that when he put in the requisite forms atop the death certificate the word came in from the bank that the account cited had been closed out two years ago and that they were not at liberty to divulge any further information without the presence of an executor.

But there is no way, in and out of memory, to tell the old man what has been done. The old man has run his final race and if he has lost it, has done so only on a technicality. When the bets were in and the machines were locked he silenced Blount and it is this, more than anything else, which the vigorous little lad holds against him; what could he have said to his father at that last moment if he had known that the old man had lied and hat all of the money had, after all, been misappro-priated and destroyed? Would he have said anything to him other than what he did say? No, Blount does not think so. Spoken out of guilt, spoken out of hatred; wormed out of disgust or too much knowledge the words would have always been the same and these were the words he said to his father:

"You son of a bitch, if I ever did get inside you, I'd pull the plug and wreck you in a second; better that I wouldn't get near you old fucking bastard."

And he knows as well what his father would have said to him if he had ever actually gotten this out: "You stu-pid bastard, I always knew that. Why do you think I called on you to do the operation?"

11

Deep in that night, the second night of the operation, Blount awakens from a thick sleep by Yancey's bed to a state of prenatural alertness. Nerves relay messages of terror; his breath comes unevenly; he feels entrapment: has the old man died in his bed and are these the warnings? He could not bear it if the old man has died for it would be the denial of his own intention—but then again, what would the difference be? The Institute has no culpability for such deaths; there would be a routine investigation and the exonerated Blount would have both the satisfaction of Yancey's death and freedom from culpability. Nevertheless, why is he peering through the dark as if that dark were to gather into the shape of a hatchet and cleave down upon him? Why is his breathing like that of a trapped dog? Blount wills himself to calm and caution, meanwhile rapidly monitoring the gross physical signs of the sleeping Yancey.

Everything is in order. Systole/diastole continue, pulse is firm at an only slightly watery 97, electrocardiogram is negative, encephelogram shows no disturbance in brain functioning. Eighty-three-year-old Yancey pounds on, as heedless in his sleep of the eternal dark as would be any athlete. He twitches, murmurs, reaches his hands toward the ceiling in an old man's embrace and draws something invisible against him. "Oh my dear," the sleeping Yancey says, "oh my *dear*, dear" and the trembling Blount is given to understand, then, that Yancey is opening up some deeper, more sentimental part of himself; there is another Yancey inside this old man, one who must have dreams of love and clutching. Not untouched by sympathetic response, Blount watches with an almost clinical interest.

"Oh I tell you, my dear," Yancey says gesticulating, "I tell you, this cannot go on much longer, I simply cannot take it." He seems to rise in the bed, pushing wires, tubing, the maze of equipment from him, his body convulsing as he reaches toward the ceiling. Blount feels panic: what will happen to him if the old man somehow wrecks the supportive systems? But that clinical detachment he has already exhibited still controls him; he rubs his hands, looks with anxiety toward the floor, but he does not lean toward Yancey nor make attempts to stop him. Let Yancey wreck the systems if he will, Blount finds himself thinking; let the old man perish in a glitter of glass, a rending of fluids, *let* the supervisors call an investigation and bring Blount before them for a true discussion of the events leading up to the disaster. Blount will have a few things to say to them as well; he does not have to put up with this kind of thing forever.

I do not have to put up with this kind of thing forever Blount murmurs and Yancey settles back, he subsides on the bed, clasping his hands in an attitude of prayer, therefore absolving his little observer of any crisis.

"Are you there son?" the old man asks quietly. "I've had a bad dream."

"I'm here," Blount says. He could rise to give Yancey the evidence of his presence but decides that this is sufficient. "Are you all right?"

"No, I am not all right, son," Yancey says. "How could I be all right? Eighty-three years old and dying and all the time you're sitting there in the dark mocking me. Don't deny it; I know your devices. You're measuring the old man for his tomb, all of you are."

"Not exactly," Blount says. Depression is a normal concurrent of the post-operative state but he feels flickers of something here that go to the center of the old man's personality. "Nobody's measuring you for anything." He leans forward, picks out Yancey's form now returned to the sheets. It would be so easy to simply reach out and strangle him. One twist, one fishlike scuttle of the trapped legs and Yancey would be under the weather forever. Tempting, easy: he would enjoy it. Blount ponders the absurdity of his position: on the one hand he does not want the old man to wreck the tubing and expire because this would create an investigation, on the other hand, he would enjoy strangling Yancey quickly under the sheets and bringing the interval to an end. How can he reconcile the two? Perhaps that is the pleasure of it, that there is no longer any consistency to his positions and he does not have to seek consistency in order to function.

"Go back to sleep," he says, the stream of dialogue continuing uninterruptedly. Say this about Blount: whatever happens he will talk smoothly, persuasively, responsively, forever. Nothing will ever quiet him.

"Measuring me for the tomb," Yancey mumbles. "I've known it from the first. You know what that bitch wants, don't you? She wants my money. Been after my money from the first even though I took her in when no one would touch her and treated her just like my own. People are no justice."

"I don't know anything about that," Blount says with clinical detachment, "why don't you rest?"

"Didn't even want me to have the operation. Tried to talk me out of it; said that there was nothing there and anyway there was too much risk. Had to sign myself in, had to force her to come along with me when all the time she had it planned. I'd be killed off in a couple of months and she'd inherit everything. Of course I straightened that one out," Yancey says, "she wouldn't have gotten a thing out of me. I'm clever enough to have made arrangements. But she could not think ahead that far; she was embraced by the fires of greed, son, and greed is a terrible emotion, don't you think? What's your opinion of greed, son?"

"I don't think that we should talk now."

"She's gotten to you too, I bet. She's probably been filling you with proper lies and deceit, begging you to do something to kill me, isn't that right son? Nothing evades me. I have dreams, terrible dreams all the time and while a man still dreams he sees."

"Please," Blount says standing, whisking the sheets into place, repressing all emotion (he will have much time to consider this later) while he tries to bring this line of discussion to an end. "This is no good for you, talking like this. You're using up energy you need to heal and anyway you'll feel differently in the morning." Solicitous, reasonable Blount! "Come now," he says, "go to sleep. I wanted to try and make the night without sedation but the important thing is for you to sleep and if we have to put in a block—"

"I knew it," Yancey mumbles, his voice trailing off a bit, "knew that you were working with her. The two of you have it planned out, don't you? I know you, you little son of a bitch; I figured that you were working with her from the first. But don't worry; the old man isn't as stupid as you think. I have friends, influence," Yancey says. "I can destroy you, just remember that, destroy you if I wish."

His voice turns off then like gas hissing through a tube is cut off by scalpel and he lies there, seemingly at perfect peace with the world, returning to sleep, leaving Blount to his own devices in the room.

Left to his own devices, Blount does the best he can. He thinks of Yancey and he thinks of Susan. He thinks of certain interesting events in his life between the ages of fourteen to sixteen which were pivotal in bringing him to this position at the present time. He runs through the greater and lesser principles of invasion as they were taught him solicitously at the Institute. He constructs a vivid scenario in which he uses the Projector for a fast reduction, clambers inside Yancey and kills him by severing the vena cava, then emerges ready in all innocence to confront the supervisors with the sad news of Yancey's final embolism. He constructs in his mind several interviews with Susan, several with the supervisors, one with the great Hulm himself in which he tries to give the human side of his predicament. All of these enable him to pass a little more of the time.

At length, however, his constructions and whimsies are exhausted. Blount finds himself sitting in the calm, hammering silence of the Institute room, looking at Yancey with uncanny perception, his mind locked to blankness, the sunlight of purpose consuming him now in splashes and wonders how long, exactly how long it will be, until he can resist Yancey's mortality no longer and what he will lose if he launches himself upon the old man without, yet, the slightest realization of motive.

"Not fair," says the damaged Blount, "not fair, not fair." But what in these circumstances is fair and what would he do if he could tell the difference? Blount finds himself thinking of his father. Had the old bastard truly wanted to die? And if that were so, would not the worst thing his son, the enemy, could have done to him was to make his way inside and force him to live?

12

"I want you to kill him," she said in the cafeteria, looking down at the floor, refusing to lift her face. "Don't ask me how, don't ask me why. He's a terrible man. He deserves to die. I know that Messengers can kill, I've studied everything about your job. They'd never find out; you'd be as safe as you could be. Haven't you ever killed one of them? I bet a lot of you have killed but of course that's not the kind of thing that gets around. I wouldn't think that the Institute would want that publicized but really what can anyone do if a Messenger decides to kill? I figure you could do it so fast that no one would even know that it had happened. And there will be money in it for you. I'll take care of you."

"The oath—" Blount said, babbling the first easy thing that came to mind, not so much in repudiation as shock. "There's an oath—"

"Oh, don't tell me about your oaths; doctors have oaths, *everybody* swears something or other when they get started in business; but that's just to protect you from being suspected, it doesn't have anything to do with reality." Finally she lifted her head, a very pretty girl, Susan Forks, not that this would do Blount any good ever and what would she say to him outside of the context of this one demand? Pretty though, pretty indeed: Blount feels a Downsider's pain knowing that this kind of girl would have never acknowledged him had he not come through the Institute and even now sees him only in the performance of her own purposes. "Don't think," she says, "that you'd get anywhere reporting this; I'd just deny every word of it. There are no witnesses—who would believe that I'd be asking you to kill my grandfather? No one would believe a word of it and they'd just have an investigation of *you*. So there's no way that you can ever report me on this, it's just the two of us. I know that you want to do it, if the price is right, and believe me I'll take care of you." She motioned to her handbag. "I have lots of money right now, you don't have to worry about getting paid. After all, how much can you people make in this miserable job? This will give you the chance to get out of it for good. I know you'll do it. I know you will."

Blount said nothing, spooning up another portion of his institutional soup, looking at Susan quietly while he worked the soup over in his mouth, then swallowed it with a gasp and stood heavily. She was drinking a glass of water and playing with a piece of bread. One thing about Susan Forks, from the beginning on, she did not seem to function on a plane of physical need.

"I've got to get back to my patient, now," Blount said, meaning this to come out authoritatively and with some finality but instead managing to sound only pompous. "I don't think we have anything more to discuss."

"Don't we?"

"No, I don't think we do. I won't do it. No Messenger would give consent to a plan for murder. Or do you think I'm crazy?"

"All Messengers are crazy," Susan Forks said meditatively, taking a piece of bread and putting it down her throat with a delicate finger or two, not bothering to swallow. "But maybe this is the wrong approach. Maybe I've been too abrupt with you; I should have put it differently."

"I said I have nothing to discuss."

"You see, it's not his money," she said, reaching out a hand, grasping Blount's wrist and guiding him ever so delicately back into his seat. "It has nothing to do with his money. I've got plenty of money. I have private reasons . . . But this really isn't getting us anywhere. I wish there was some way that I could convince you . . ."

"There's no way," Blount said. "No way at all."

As he leaned toward the girl, trying (he believed) to convince her with the intensity of his position, he could feel himself caught by some aspect of her which he could not explain nor, for that matter, wish to explain: there she was, a girl of twenty-three this Susan Forks, granddaughter of Yancey, a man whom Blount had already decided to murder, asking that murder be committed again. But it was not this Blount thought of as he looked into her eyes, not thoughts of murder or even of the irony of double-motives; no, he was caught by something else about this girl and what it was was something too profound for the poor Messenger to seize; it might have been her face, an expression around the eyes which reminded him of nothing so much as his poor father, it might have been the lines descending from those eyes to the nose and then the open, pouting smile of the mouth as she caved in under his realization; passing his gaze downward Blount found himself staring at her body in a detached but fascinated way: the suspicion of breasts under her simple, unelaborate robes, the hint of thighs rising underneath the table; maybe the heat of the girl itself enveloping him like a shroud and oh Blount was in extremis, gentlemen! you must bear with him, a man of small moods and passions (although barely able to enact them) like so many of you he found himself caught and pinned by this girl's gaze, winking and twinkling of her eyelids then and she reached across the table to seize the faint and fluttering wrist of the little Messenger in a grip firm and unyielding like the grip with which his father had taken him into the Institute:

"You'll do it," she said to him then, seeing something. "You're going to do it, aren't you?"

"No. No."

"Yes. Yes you are," she said, squeezing and squeezing and her face took on many colors . . . but perhaps these were only the tears springing in and out of Blount's eyes as he gazed upon her, causing Susan to appear in many-hued shades as she overtook the circle of vision. "You're going to do it! Do you know why? Do you?"

"I will not," he said. "This is monstrous. The man is eighty-three years old; he has done nothing—"

"You want to do it," she said. "You want to murder him. You want to make me happy, and you know I won't be happy unless you do it. You're going to make me happy," she said, her fingers working their way up and down his arm, full of messages and tapping, "very happy. If you make me happy, I'll make you happy."

Her fingernails touched, spread open on her breast. "Watch me," she said, "just watch me," and then she stood, left the table in a rush and walked rapidly from the cafeteria under Blount's fascinated gaze which seemed to devolve into a narrower and narrower line of insight until finally as she passed through a door he was looking at her back, at her buttocks, at her right buttock, at a small arc of her right buttock, pale as a moon beneath, emitting shafts of energy that might have been pained as Blount leaned over the table and howled and howled (but quietly, not to bring down perdition at once) with the rage of it, a rage that might have been laughter. Because in the fantasies on her he had had it all wrong after all: she understood nothing. She thought he functioned from common motives. She thought he was a man.

13

Graduation day at the Institute: a taped message from the Director. The tape must be very old; Hulm is seen at a more youthful period of his life in film spliced unevenly, opening up cracks and wrinkles which could not occur on that young vigorous frame. The Director is seen sitting at his ease behind a desk, talking to an interviewer who is invisible; after a while, the sheer energy and conviction of the Director drive him to a restless standing posture and he stalks back and forth behind the desk, unevenly, but always in the fullest command of himself.

"Great obligation," the Director says (the coordination of the sound track with the film is rather poor and it is difficult to make out the words; also synchronization lapses completely at times so that the Director appears to be talking vigorously when it is the interviewer who is asking a question. "Tremendous spirit, cycles of training, dedication to humanity. All things together, taken as they are one by one, never such a group of men. Dedication, commitment, passion, justice," the Director says, pacing so vigorously that watery paintings on the wall behind him actually jiggle, "obsession, compulsion, knife, Institute."

Blount, leaning forward in his chair in the fifth row center (there, we can see him now, the boom camera comes in subtly and we can see his parched little face, frozen with attention, swallowing up the screen) takes it all in at some level of subconscious motive, casting surreptitious glances toward the exits now and then and trying to time the film. How long can it be? How long could the Director have been talking? It seems to have been going on for hours.

In the hall, little Messengers whistle and mumble amongst themselves while the film grinds on. Three hundred and fifteen of them being graduated today, one of the largest classes in the history of the Institute and one of the most tragic as well since no less than five hundred and twelve of their original number have fallen by the wayside during the struggle for the diploma and the drill. Some have sneaked from the Institute's quarters at night between bedchecks (which become more casual in the later years) and have never been heard of again; others have risen in their classes to assault Instructors with their little fists. Some have been caught in the act of trying to murder a test-case, one could not find an exit from a cadaver in time and exploded the cadaver to a distance of three hundred feet, causing himself fatal cerebral energies. Several of the Messengers have been withdrawn from the Institute by legal action of their families, one of them was caught in the act of destroying a Projector. Three of the prospective Messengers have been intercepted during a crazed rotor flight the purpose of which was somehow to find the secret entrance into the secret quarters of the great Director Hulm himself and assassinate him.

On the other hand, many of the Messengers have been disqualified for simple failure of nerve or technique. Almost a hundred have proven too clumsy to operate the gear inside the body, a hundred or so more for lacking the visual acuity to move around under the poor lighting conditions of the cavity. It is not to be thought then that Blount's class is one distinguished by psychopathic tendencies or gross abnormalities of any other kind; the fact is that the percentage of those being forced to drop because of bizarre activities has been lower than the norm. Most of the Messengers resigned, it seems, are simply in capable, no mystique to it. They have all been returned to Downside except for the occasional scattering of lunatics who came from a less disadvantaged set of areas, thinking that being a Messenger would make for an interesting career.

"Facility, application, wonder," the Director babbles from the screen and the lights at last go up, that portion of the ceremony dealing with artifacts or ancient wonders at last having been concluded and now a murmur of sheer anticipation or perhaps it is horror (it is so difficult to tell) begins to build among the Messengers who realize that the truly consequential portion of the program is being reached; now is the time for the actual taking of the oath, the awarding of the diplomas, the passing out of the ceremonial drills. Deep from his perch in the fifth row center Blount meditates as to whether the proper time has yet come for his announcement or whether he should wait. He decides that he will wait; the time has not quite come around and from a certain psychological point of view it would be best not to betray his purposes with a premature expostulation. No, he will wait until the attention of the audience has been fully deflected upon the interesting and profound ceremonies taking place upon the physical stage and then he will strike.

Blount puts his little hands on wasted knees, peers left and right, looking upon the faces of his fellow Messengers. Most of them he will never see again (he fervently hopes that this will be the case); they will be dispersed to Institutes throughout this wondrous land, some of them will be assigned to the overseas subsidiaries which are just building, a few will be detained in the great Center itself for advanced training and research. From Kentucky to Kansas, from Illinois to California the graduating class of the Institute will disperse never to be huddled in the same room again. Some of them will fulfill their enlistments quietly and leave at the end of the five-year period, their savings nestled away carefully to sustain them as they strike a new life-style, others will not have been as cautious or fearful of their condition and will have no savings, therefore being forced to re-enlist for another five-year period. It is this percentage, about fifty percent of the total Blount has been told, which will be in real trouble because Messengers are not allowed to serve beyond ten years, losing their skill of hand or strength of stomach rapidly after the age of thirty and there is no telling what will happen to aging Messengers who are denied that one last enlistment which would set them straight. Some of them will go straight to suicide of course and others will be found in the streets around the Institutes begging relatives of patients for alms as conscience-money but neither suicide nor begging are entirely satisfactory because there is little future in them. Blount finds himself thinking of the fate of old Messengers somewhat idly: exactly what does become of that proportion of them who have made no plans and have no alternatives? They can stay in the Institutes, a very few of them of course, performing routine tasks as orderlies, some of them are employed by the training Center to act as experimentation fields for very junior students . . . but no, Blount decides shuddering, this is completely impossible; he will not think of that at all. He must be one of the Messengers who lives in penury for five years, savaging his instincts over and over again for the price of a little security and when he leaves at the end of the five years it will be with the ability to start an entirely new life. He can if he is careful save two hundred thousand dollars; wisely and carefully invested he can almost get along on this . . . if he is willing to live miserably.

But this will not work out either. Blount knows, even as he ponders these alternatives for the twelfth or fifteenth time that he is merely deluding himself. There are no old Messengers, no ex-Messengers rocking themselves into senility and quiet on their interest; there are only young Messengers and beginning Messengers and the recently retired. What happens to Messengers after the age of thirty-five is an area which has remained almost totally unexplored both within the Institutes and in the popular press and there has been little impetus to have the veil lifted. In fact no one, least of all young Messengers, is interested. Not for Blount the simple gray years of peace between his profession and death; not for Blount long, streaked afternoons in the bars or drug palaces or the Arena rambling in memory through small parcels of his life; Blount has known from the very beginning that it would never be this way. Not for him. No, he has thought only in terms of spectacular culminations, wild thrashings, multi-hued disasters, confrontations and collisions which will imprint the wee outlines of his sinewy figure deep upon the face of his time.

Growing up in Downside has contributed to this sense of calamitous destiny but it is not only that experience (for many Downsiders, Blount reflects, have quite a neutral sense of themselves and, in fact, enjoy being beaten) which has made him this way; it has been the careful and chilling education which his father had worked out for him during the so-called formative years.

The Systems of his father have cultivated within Blount a sense of the wild possibilities of life, all of them laid over a fabric of recurring disaster: time and again, seeing his father in the possession of an Ultimate Insight only to be rolled down again and again into humility and hopelessness, Blount found himself approaching the verge of the secret of all existence and the secret was simply this; nothing made any sense at all. Order would collapse, systems would prove their futility, a carefully contrived superstructure would totter and collapse in flames and this outcome simply had nothing to do with human effort: the systems were certainly sound, they were promising, they were workable, in the abstract they would function again and again . . . it was only, as a matter of fact, in their application that they would prove no more capable of changing the face of the Downsider's life than Blount's father himself.

Maiden colts would always beat maiden fillies in a mixed race but then again, they might not and the exact percentage of failure would cancel out the amount of risk which Blount senior had calculated he could manage; Blount had been through many nights with his father, nights of wild and ascending adventure during which a new system would be given its final testing preparatory to being sent on its shy course the next day, nights in which his father had babbled and chuckled as amiably as any landlord of Downside; and Blount had gone through the afternoons too, the afternoons one after the other when it would happen to be that the new systems had tiny but irreparable flaws. He had seen the shift of his father's moods as somehow embracing the phases of the Moon, changes of the seasons, curvature of the Earth and in seeing again and again his father reenact these cycles Blount had lost that simple faith in consistency which could be the Downsider's only salvation . . . that there was a reason for him to be in this condition and if he would only give the reason a lifetime to sort itself out, everything would come into focus. Blount no longer believed this.

He no longer believed this; he sat in the fifth row center at the Institute graduation a man disabused by observation of everything in which he could have believed and had managed to convince himself that at some strategic point, the absolutely right moment of the ceremony, he would leap to a posture of attention and, explaining to all assembled precisely why he had come to this conclusion, utter terrible threats against the Institute and its staff and then walk out. He knew that there would be no retaliation; the graduation ceremonies were on film and camera and anyway it would hardly be worth their while to make a series of sensational charges which could only give publicity to this point of view. No, they would let him walk out and abandon his enlistment and Blount would at least have the satisfaction of knowing that at the proper moment he had done all he could to repudiate his life . . . no matter how little he could effect it.

So now as the ceremony went on, as the Naming of Names began and then the ritual of the Forty-Five Ways preparatory to the formal administration of the Oath, Blount sat in his little seat clasping his little hands while his little knees trembled: should he do it now? He had more or less phrased in mind what he wanted to say.

"*You bastards,*" he wanted to point out, "*you dirty sons of bitches, you lied to us, you're lying to us right now. You're using the irrevocable patents to make yourselves rich from a process which should be available to everyone and instead are offered only to that part of the population, the rich bastards, which almost by definition are the least worthy of salvation; you are holding onto a process which could be one of the greatest blessings in the history of Mankind only to use it to prolong lives already lived too long, lives built on inheritance or avarice and it is time that the lie be told, that the horror be seen clear. You have built up all of this mystery around the Projector and the Messengers because the simple truth, the simple patent could be applied to any who ask for it at almost no cost other than the time of the Messenger, and the Messenger himself is a manual laborer. The Forty-Five Points, the four years of training, all of the experimentation and pathways is so much garbage. Anyone with a steady eye, a blind mind and good hands could do this job—for a few weeks. And then he'd go crazy. But if you'd release the patents you wouldn't need a corps of Messengers; everybody could do his share.*"

Does Blount really mean this?

Yes, he really means it. He is at this stage of his life an intensely serious young man for all of his laughable stature, a man of set opinions and clear apprehension, a man who feels that he has indeed found the answers, however limited, which will apply to his situation: how can he be condemned? Hypocrisy motivates him not, greed is extraneous; by saying what he intends to say publicly his career will be ended, his hopes smashed; he will be a Downsider forever. Nevertheless, even accepting all of this, Blount feels his responsibilities keenly: someone must be told about this. It is one thing for the Messengers in training to grumble and mumble these possibilities amongst themselves; it is another to confront the terror squarely.

I'm going to do it, Blount murmurs, *I am really going to do it* and decides that this is the time: now, no further delays, he urges his tiny knees to lock and lift him upwards, passes commands toward speech through his delicate nervous system and out to the vocal cords and as Messengers to the right and left of him begin to notice his behavior, turning subtly to the side to observe the struggles of Blount he opens his mouth and to the best of his ability, he begins to speak.

"I accept," Blount says, his voice not booming but rather a teeny-tiny whine backed deep in his throat. "Oh, my God, I accept this, accept all of it!"

What the hell is he saying? Nevertheless he goes on: "I accept, oh my Lord, yes, I accept the bowels, accept the body, accept the bloodstream, accept my condition." Wringing his hands, quite astonished by his conduct but with a strange sense of peace he re-seats himself. Messengers surrounding him return their attention to the stage. Remarkably, he has made very little impression of any sort.

"Accept, accept," the damaged Blount murmurs, feeling the acceptance working its way from the pit of the stomach upwards and through various layers. "Oh, my God, I accept," and returns his attention to the stage where the vast Naming of Names is continuing, the stage blazing with light, the dark music of the ceremony whining from hidden speakers. No one has noticed him. No one has heard. He rubs his palms together thinking of this, of the great lessons that he has learned today and passes into a cold, empty tube of time in which there is no sense of chronology, his mind completely blanked except for certain images of his father's face which as if on the spokes of a wheel, whirl before him in different attitudes. Smiles, intensity, pathos, tears, longing he sees on the multiple images of his father's face and at last his name is called and Blount bounds to the stage to receive his commission and as he does this he feels his tiny heart beating in his breast: oh he is grateful, grateful, grateful!

14

Yancey, feeling stronger, slightly ambulatory, leans toward Blount from his chair with a cunning and complicated expression. "I know why you like this job, lad," he says, leering, "and why you're in need of salvation—you enjoy it! You enjoy getting inside people, poking around swinishly, fooling around with parts of their bodies. You are beyond salvation, son, because you have violated the Temple of the Holy Spirit and nothing can save you unless you repent."

"If I hadn't gone inside," Blount said—he has no business arguing with Yancey, he knows this, futile and pointless but he has been goaded past his little limits—"if I hadn't gone inside you, you would have died, don't you understand that?"

"How do you know?"

"How do I know? The *charts*—"

"You invent the questions that will give you the answers you seek, lad; your charts are prepared to foregone conclusions. No, you have no way of knowing this; there might have been nothing inside me. But the curse does not fall upon me for this violation," Yancey says, folding his hands and leaning back, almost at ease, "but upon you. I was merely the inert focus of your tormented desires. You are in very serious trouble, son. You are going to burn unredeemed in hellfire for centuries whereas those who respect the essential mysteries will live forever."

"Who?" Blount says, choking a little with the fury of it: is Yancey being deliberately obtuse as a scheme for

Blount to reveal his purposes at once or is the old man really this stupid? "Who put you in this Institute to begin with? I didn't do it. No one forced you to come. You came of your own decision—"

"Now *you* know," Yancey says ever so softly, neatly adjusting his gown around him and rubbing his palms with contentment, "you know that that is not the point, son. Human frailty and human consequences are entirely separate and can never be compared. I have devoted my lifetime to studying this and similar issues and your arguments will hold no weight at all. I am getting a little tired, son. I do not wish to continue this conversation. You can help me back into the bed."

"You did this," Blount says pointlessly. "Not me—"

"That is not so. You did everything. Everything that happens to you you caused yourself. I was merely here, lad. You will please help me back into the bed; I do not want to repeat myself."

Slowly, Blount approaches the old man, puts his hands upon his arms, squeezes, lifts. He could break the old man open in the chair, smash him like kindling and leave the splinters in a tumble for the staff to retrieve later. He could, for that matter, simply strangle Yancey undramatically in the chair and arrange details afterward so that it would look like a cerebral accident. *There is no reason,* he thinks, *no reason to be circuitous*; why can he simply not come to the point and do what he must? Well, this is not the first time Blount has asked himself this question; it is hardly an area worth pursuit. He supposes that he will not do what he simply must do because if he killed the old man unsubtly and face to face in this manner he would not only take chances which he does not want to at this point (Blount it must be said cherishes what he thinks of as his freedom) but furthermore, nothing important would be resolved. He still does not understand, understand exactly what Yancey has touched him through, and until he does murder would only function to close off a good avenue of discovery.

Help him back to the bed then. Blount puts a hand on the old man's shoulders, heaves, lifts, poises and escorts him, grunting back to the bed. Yancey falls in the dead-center of the sheets with a sigh and a splatter, curving his body into a question mark and snuggling under those sheets for comfort. He draws them up against his cheek, rubs the cheek, his eyes becoming wide with submission. How could Blount want to kill such a helpless old man? How could Blount find anything which this specter said to him maddening? Something must have happened to his mind; surely he cannot see menace in this pitiful old bugger. . . .

Yes he can.

"I can save you, lad," Yancey says hoarsely, "you can yet be saved."

"Rest now."

"No," Yancey says, extending a forefinger and beckoning Blount in close. "I am really serious. Do you think that I showed you the heart of your darkness merely to abandon you Godless on the beach? Do you not think that I offer you salvation as well, son? It would be cruel and preposterous if I offered you the one without the other. Come here."

Blount backs away, sprawls over the chair, falls into it uncomfortably, arranging his person. "I don't want to hear it anymore," he says. "You must leave me alone."

"I knew you could not ignore me forever. Don't stay away from me now. Come. Come in." Yancey draws the sheets down to his waist, with much huffing and puffing, manages a seating posture and makes Blount a grim gesture of invitation. "Come here," he says, and Blount comes, moving off the chair as transfixed, scuttling to the side of the bed, feeling himself drawn into Yancey. Odors and colors come off the old man's body; looking away from Blount now in profile he might be a saint after all, yes, the old bugger might be a saint, the lines of his face creased toward resignation, a strange, holy light peeping shyly within. Blount feels a hand clap like a bell on his shoulder.

"You must pray," Yancey says, "you must pray for remission of your awful deeds, the corruption carried within your seed by those gross improprieties. I will teach you the rituals and you will perform them."

"Pray to whom?"

"It does not matter," Yancey says. "The focus of the prayer is the prayer itself, the receptacle is immaterial. Pray to God if you will, or to the Devil. The meaning is in the prayer. Ask for remission. Confess your inequities."

The hand tightens on Blount. "You really ought to get started on that now, son; it's already very late for you."

The hand moves upward, passes across his shoulder blades, nestles on the nape of Blount's little neck. He feels the fingers twitching, as if in passion or reminiscence. Indeed, was this the secret all the time? Has he finally resolved Yancey's motives: does the old bugger simply want Blount to swaddle with him under the sheets and make deep confession?

"Now, son," Yancey says, "it's time to make your confession and prayer."

Insane. What if an attendant were to walk through the door to see them grouped so intimately under the sheets; what if Susan were to see what her grandfather and his Messenger were up to now? Would Blount have a chance? Is there any way that he could get out of this? What would he say to the hospital staff; how would he properly defend his position? Yet, at the same time, it is oddly comfortable being in this posture with Yancey; the old man's clean body radiates no odors now, his muscles betray no nervousness; ancient memories occur to Blount of nights in Downside when he was young and could not sleep, hurtling under the sheets with his father.

"Grant me peace for I have sinned," Yancey says.

"Grant me peace for I have sinned."

"Grant me peace for I have known the call of the flesh and have entered upon the body corrupt and with unclean hands."

"Grant me peace for I have known the call of the flesh and have entered upon the body corrupt and with unclean flesh."

"Unclean hands, son."

"Unclean hands."

"I have known pride and the lusts of the heretic."

"I have known pride and the lusts of the heretic."

"And I plead for your forgiveness."

"And I plead for your forgiveness."

"That's enough for now, son," Yancey says. "That's a beginning for today. I don't want you to do too much at one time. Meditate upon what you have said and on the meaning of those words and then later we'll say them again and some more. Would you get out of the bed now, lad? I'm tired and I find your presence disgusting. It's one thing to try to help you but I just can't take any more of this."

Now. It would be so easy now. Blount could even make it look like an accident. Sudden thrashings of the patient in the bed, a rush to defend him from self-inflicted damage, poor placement of limbs in the excitement, a complete loss of balance and Blount, falling awkwardly, crushed the life out of the helpless patient before he could make a move in defense. The Higher Board would clear it after a simple investigation and there certainly would be no pressure for further explorations by the nearest living relative.

But Blount cannot do it. He can, in fact, do nothing, so burdened has he become by the content of Yancey's prayer. He disengages from the bed, from the patient (if an orderly or doctor had peered in, what would they have thought of this posture?) and staggers away, toward the mirror over the basin, looking there to see if his features have been altered. Solemnly he looks back upon himself . . . unchanged. Nothing will ever change him. Nothing will happen to convey from Blount the burden of himself.

Yancey's breathing is peaceful and even. The old man is well on the way to recovery, speeded for all Blount knows by his own prayer and Blount, alone in the room has nothing. *Grant me peace for I have known the call of the flesh and have entered upon the body corrupt and with unclean flesh. Unclean hands. Have entered upon the body with unclean hands. Have known the pride and the lusts of the heretic. And plead for your forgiveness . . .*

Whose forgiveness? Blount wonders. Who is in that position?

15

He thinks that he can see it all. Susan lies upon the bed naked, an old, cold, bold smile, naked breasts upthrusting, thighs heaving, her mound already wet with suggestion, and Yancey, also naked, stands to one side looking down upon her, licking his lips and trying to will his eighty-three-year-old joint to erection. Sometimes it will function and sometimes it will not, but more and more as he ages the functioning of his prick seems to be utterly outside of his control: like a thirteen-year-old he will sometimes find himself with enormous erections when there is no possibility of using them and then again, as now with his granddaughter, he is flaccid in the presence of a living, necessitous female. Maddening, maddening: it would make a religious fanatic out of any man, cause him to displace motives and reasons upon some detached force which can only overpower him but nevertheless Yancey will not give up the ship, not while there is life in those old limbs, and besides, the girl will do anything that he asks. She has no position in the matter; she can only be enacted upon by him time and again, her options are limited, her purposes fixed and so Yancey at least does not have to incur fear or shame. Anything that he does to her will still control the situation. So slowly, slowly then he lowers himself upon her, hands and knees spreading and flexed as he surrounds her body and bending down to give her neck the gentlest of bites and kisses, rubs his detumescence against her thigh, feels himself stretching, longing to greet her then but does not know whether this is a stretching of the prick or spirit, maybe a little bit of both he concludes cunningly as he locks himself into her, maybe a little bit of both; in any event penetration has been made and his crinkled, wrinkled surface blends itself against hers, his granddaughter rears up, opening fully against him and he settles into a deeper level, wetness, recrimination, memory overtaking him as Yancey returns to the most primitive gestures of all and eighty-three years old or more bends to nibble on her breasts, ingesting a nipple, a child's swoon as he feeds upon her and then to more serious business, huffing and puffing, humping and jumping on the sheets. He thinks that he is going to be able to come. It is always difficult to tell about these matters and more and more the body now is the betrayer of purposes but as far as he can test from all known reserves and retrospect he will succeed this time. Something seems to be moving in the tubing and ligaments of old Yancey and he does not think that it is indigestion. Not this time. No sir indeed, from the deepest reservoirs of the human spirit, Yancey is actually fucking her.

He is really doing it! Never will they say that eighty-three is hopeless or dead, not while old Yancey here is still able to do it. His contemporaries lie in graveyards or senescence; Yancey alone has prevailed over chronology to come to this equivocal but real victory. It is a shame that it is a kind of incest he is performing—although granddaughter really is a distant relation and he had barely known her mother, that bitch at all; in fact once or twice he had doubted parentage, not that you wanted to fight about things like that when you had a ministry to protect and all kinds of things going on the side for you as well—so fuck it, fuck the bitch; if she wasn't his own daughter she could have the line of descent anyway and welcome to it but she had died thirty years ago now or was it thirty-five? no it couldn't be that long ago, Susan being only twenty-three, well make it twenty anyway, a hell of a long time ago whatever it was—so let it all be; what matters is that there is a woman in his bed and he is actually, actually doing it to her. Who would have believed it? Fifty years ago would he have known or cared that he might come to a condition like this? He had never really planned his future, that was one of the problems. The hell with it. Give it to her good. Yancey pumps and pumps, realizes behind his closed eyelids that he has indeed been pumping for a very long time, his mind trailing off in small filaments of thought that have nothing to do with concentrating on the issue at hand. If he does not stop this and concentrate he will lose the erection, will definitely not come and what then? All of this will have been a waste.

"Temple of the holy spirit, baby," he whispers to his granddaughter, biting on an ear, squeezing her nipples in the tight little space between their bellies.

"The flesh and the blood and the spirit," she heaves back at him, automatically making a better, tighter fit, except that he is definitely losing his erection, no question about it now, down to half a rod or less, slipping outside of her. He feels cool breezes on his genitals, the damp of futility. Too small. Nothing. He has burnt out.

"Goddamn it you bitch!" he says, turning it against her as he would surely have to. "What the hell is wrong with you?" and squeezes her nipples harder, she cries, he groans, she mutters with pain as he brings in the pressure, hatred in the squeezes now because she has taunted and taunted him with her woman's body only at the end being unable to bring him on. If she had not aroused him with her body he would not have to face the failure now; he could have resigned to the peace and hopeless dignity of the old man if she were not always around there to mock and excite him. *He could kill her.*

Not to think of that now Yancey, he reminds himself; he has been there before, has felt the murder in his belly, the tightness of the killer in his hands and if he does not control himself through these rages he is, one of these times, going to do her serious damage and no mistake about it. Or thrust himself into a stroke with all of this blockage of energy. But how to stop? how to stop? she is still underneath him, her face open and streaked with tears, her little hands grasping and rasping at him, crying deep from her throat, turning her head from side to side as he pounds at her. No matter what he does, no matter what happens or fails to happen, she has never denied him, she has never been the one to break the connection and she will not do it this time either. Call it fear or love, reluctance or dependence, once underneath him she will not release the hold and Yancey, seeing this, does not know whether it vaults his feeling to a new level or instead only increases his rage: she will not allow him to fail discreetly. His futility, his hopelessness must be expressed to its longest and deepest point and only when he is willing to quit, fall off her and stagger away to his own bedroom, only then will she get off of her back and resume her own life. The challenge is as deep as the submission; there is absolutely nothing that he can do about it. Flailing away, Yancey feels like a little dot upon her thigh. He knows that he has failed again. He relents. He stops.

"Damn bitch," he says. "You're all the same." Although the point of this remark at least rather evades him: of course they are all the same, and so is he for that matter.

"Just you remember," he says, drawing up his knees and forcing himself to a precarious balance, then with an agility which costs him almost all equilibrium, swings his feet to the floor and rapidly stands, staggers into a wall, heads toward the door, "just remember that you won't get away with this. It's my life just as much as it's yours until I'm dead and not a moment sooner and you'll be damned if you'll change the thing until that happens. And if you don't watch it, I'll take you with me."

He walks out. Susan has said nothing. Susan, in fact,

has thought nothing for the last twenty-five minutes, being too involved instead with blank considerations of the walls, the floor, the ceiling (constantly) and the filamentation of the lamps as they burn through her eyelids. Thought will never get her through these exercises, only its obverse will. Now at last she allows herself to think again, opening herself up and emotion fills her like air rushing into a vacuum, she digs away at her features with hard little fingernails, trying to control herself. Hysteria will get her nowhere; calm everywhere. This cannot go on. It simply cannot go on much longer. She cannot take this. There must come an end to it.

She pivots on her stomach, raising her delicate buttocks slightly to the ceiling as had Yancey over her, hunched over an imaginary vision on the bed. She puts her face against the pillow, trying to make that vision solid. She paints the outlines of the vision in her mind: the delicate grave features, the skillful little hands, the suffering eyes that have glimpsed horrors worse than hers and thus will survive it. She creates the vision for herself again as she has so many times, the vision five feet one and full of fun, scurrying in the body's doom, hot on the trail of an infection. She addresses this vision. She prays to it.

"Oh please help me!" she says. "Grant me release, grant me assistance." And the vision, heaped in flames, nods and winks and says that he will do his best as those flames of departure take him away. He kisses her brow, touches her cheeks, murmurs of faith and it is this and only this which sustains Susan in the sleep that takes her then and the next night as well and the next after that.

And the day after *that* on his routine six-month medical, Yancey gets the first indications from the laboratory assistants of his developing tumor.

16

In the little cubicle at the Institute which is his living quarters, Blount keeps the hulk of the Priest which at the Arena he destroyed. Why not? why should he not keep it? the Priest was, they said, damaged and destroyed solely because of Blount's irresponsibility and twelve hundred and fifteen depreciated dollars had to be settled on its coils. For twelve hundred and fifteen dollars, Blount thought, the least that they could do was to give him the Priest; why not indeed? they said but cartage was Blount's responsibility and they would not be liable for any electric shocks or other injuries the wee lad might incur by manipulating the ruined object. So Blount paid another three hundred and thirty dollars for transport as well as signing a waiver specifically relieving the Arena of all further rights or responsibilities. He set up the Priest against one bare wall of the room, the wall facing the entrance where it proceeded to dominate his quarters . . . as well it should have since Blount had nothing else to his name other than a bureau and a closet, neither of them filled with personal materials. He had no personal materials. He had no personal life.

But he had the Priest; the Priest and he had a relationship and although Blount would never foolishly attempt to operate the machine, its sheer presence there, mute, still-life as an artifact, was sufficient to give him at odd moments a sensation of power, at all times a sensation of peace. Somewhere within the Priest even if he could not get at them, all the answers lay, the full set of explanations to the universe and his own awful predicament which would make everything clear. The Priest, vintage 1993, knew everything Blount decided (he had never respected the instrument so much as after he had wrecked it) and just to be in the presence of the answers was good enough. Well, almost good enough. Sometimes he felt impelled to talk to it.

He feels impelled now. His dialogues with the Priest (always one-sided) are erratic; he will say nothing to the machine for days, then again he will become voluble and spend hours in intense consultation with the machine, bringing it up to date in the various necessary aspects of Blount's life, peppering the machine with little advisements and stray recollections, his stream-of-consciousness almost uncontrollable during these times of communion with the Priest . . . but then again, dissatisfied, Blount will lapse into silence, have nothing to say to the Priest for as long as a week, trying to get away from what he knows in his better moments to be the insane pursuit of taking the machine as seriously as he takes himself. He is not in such an interval now, however; he has indeed a lunatic urge to tell the Priest everything and then relying upon the dead gearing, to cue it in for an answer. What will happen? most likely nothing, the device is disassembled inside, all of its electrodes and connections dead but then again the Priest may have been holding within itself one last insight or absolution which he will be able to spring loose. It is worth trying; he has arranged with the nursing staff for three hours of blank time, his patient being under sedation for the night, and he intends to use this time as diligently as possible toward the making of the final decision because Yancey is scheduled for release on the day after tomorrow, early. The medical staff have approved this release; the old man is gaining in strength and courage all the time and fluoroscopy shows no hint of metasteses. Blount has done his work well. Whatever his psychic difficulties, accept this: he does his work competently and he often enjoys it. Now, on the precipice of undoing his wonderful work, Blount feels that he needs consultation. He needs the advice of the Priest, if only by implication.

"Excuse me," the delicate little lad says, closing the door and bolting it, hammering a chair into place then to safeguard his security, divesting himself of all his robes and seating himself naked before the Priest. "I have something of a problem and need your advice. Should I kill the old son of a bitch or would this be a false remission? What do you think?"

This does not seem to make a great deal of sense to Blount, now that he thinks of it—he has given the confessor none of the background, has opened *in medias res* in a fashion which would bedazzle even a youthful Priest . . . but then again, is this not the point of the confessional? What does the confessor need to know of background?

"I can't stand it anymore," Blount says. "I mean I really can't stand it anymore. But on the other hand I'm afraid that I'll simply never get away with it and I couldn't stand that. I have a horror of confinement, of closed places, of delimitation. Surely you can understand this."

"Of course I can," the Priest says (often it talks back to Blount but only in an internal way, meaning that Blount in effect is talking to himself; but this has never bothered the wee fellow since he knows that insanity is merely another way of coming to terms with the environment in a healthy fashion), "I can understand very much. Confess and be blessed. Bless and be saved. You say you want to kill the old man do you? Remarkable, remarkable; he's eighty-three and will die within a few years on his own. You ought to survive him by fifty, son. Of course, that isn't the whole story, is it?"

"No," Blount says. "Not exactly. Of course it isn't. If it was just a question of survival, of mortality—"

"Then it's more direct. *You* want to be the agent of his death."

"Exactly. That's exactly right."

"Confess and be blessed. Seek remission for all of your sins."

"But I don't want remission, you see," Blount points out reasonably. "I simply want to enact them. What's wrong with that?"

"That's unreasonable. That is not the kind of thinking which is characteristic of you, Blount. You have hardly achieved the distinguished position you've managed in life with thinking of that sort."

"That's true," Blount says, "that's very true."

He enjoys his discussions with the Priest. More than anything else they seem to complement certain directions in his thinking, tend to render concrete the amorphous, giving comfort, in fact, to his weaknesses. If the Priest tends to miss certain ironies while seizing ignorantly upon superficialities, that does not have to injure their relationship; it simply means that Blount must concentrate the more closely to hold up not only his end of the discussion but the Priest's. Besides, it gives him the feeling that he is at least intellectually in control of his situation, which is not to be minimized at this stage of his life.

"Nevertheless, I'm entitled to my position, am I not? I want to kill the old bastard, I really do."

"The world is full of such motives. Most of them are not enacted."

"The world is also filled with murders."

"Ah," the Priest says, "this is true. But there are many less murders than motives, many less murderers than impulses."

"I want to be among the elect."

"So be among the elect," the Priest says. Inanimate as it is, it appears to shrug delicately. "Go ahead and kill the old bastard and then come here for penance. See if I care. It's your life, Blount."

"Don't make it so easy. That's not your role."

"I'm only giving you what you want."

"How do you know what I want until I tell you?"

"You told me," the Priest points out. "You told me that you wanted to murder Yancey. So all I say is go ahead and do it. I can't stop you. No one can stop you. From the very beginning it's been your life, Blount. No one is living it but you. All of the options, all of the choices, were always yours. So go on and perform; then come to me."

"What options did I have? What options did I ever have? Coming out from Downside—"

"I'm not really here to listen to you whine, Blount. That's definitely not my role and I'm quite filled with your disgusting self-pity. If you can't find a better line to take—"

"But what choices do I have? What choices did I ever have? I never had an option in my life."

"You could have dropped out of the Institute."

"And gone where?"

"You could have performed the operation on your father," the Priest says. "Now that's a point. Nothing was stopping you, you know, from volunteering to go inside and try to clean him out. Actually, the fact is and you'd better face this, you've been racked by guilt for months and months for letting him die. You think that maybe you should have tried to save him. But instead of admitting your guilt you're thinking of killing Yancey, which will prove that all the time you were right because you're nothing but a killer."

"That's the cheapest thing I ever heard in my life." Blount says. "Of all the disgusting, stupid lines of argument—"

"You know it's the truth. That's why you don't like it."

"The old man was terminal. It was no filaments. Nothing could have saved him; it was no job for a Messenger."

"So you've convinced yourself."

"I don't want to talk about this anymore. Keep quiet."

"You started."

"So I started. I'm finishing. No more. No more of this."

"Wake up, Blount," the Priest murmurs. "You're putting yourself into an impossible position. Soon you'll be so convinced you're right that you won't be able to do anything. Nothing at all. Just remember that."

"He was terminal. I told you that. There was something the size of a baseball in his small intestine. It was no job for me!"

"Quiet, Blount," the Priest says. "You're shouting."

"I'm not shouting. I'm trying to make you understand—"

"No more," the Priest says. "It's quite futile to attempt to discuss anything with you in this state. I will say no more."

And it says no more, switching itself to a lower gear then, standing square and innocent in the line of Blount's vision, the dialogue at an end.

Blount rubs his forehead and mutters with anger. If he had not already gone through this with the Priest he might attack it, kick the damned machine to splinters now, and quiet that maddening, reasonable voice forever. But he knows that this time there will be no shutting off of that voice for it emanates from within a different area entirely and the means to excise it are out of Blount's hands. Everything is now out of his hands.

He contents himself with administering a few kicks to the machine, stubbing his toe, and then collapses on his bed in an attitude of total dejection, too drained to even stretch out and let himself go to sleep. If he collapses into sleep he will lose the fine, tight line of persuasion which has brought him to this point; everything may go away from him and he may awaken numb to look at the Priest with stricken eyes and wonder where he could have ever suffered the passion to care. No, at all costs his emotional state must be preserved; Blount has been walking a difficult, tense line for many days now but if the alternative is to drop it completely, all will slide away from him and Yancey will walk out of the Institute, eighty-three years old and healthy, ready to return to his life and this would be unspeakable.

Stay awake then, maintain the tensions and try to work through to conclusions. Twelve hours until Yancey's discharge. What is Blount going to do? Exactly what is on this twenty-two-year-old youth's mind?

"You son of a bitch; you can't do this to me," Blount says to the Priest, but almost caressingly. He is, after all, quite fond of the device. In a profound sense it might be said that he owes it everything. In another sense, perhaps, it might be said that he owes the Priest nothing since the Priest is responsible, as much as any other factor, for his present condition. Who knows? One thing is clear and that is that the relationships here are profound, complicated and difficult. Blount would never have conceived that he would have fallen into a network of possibility so tenuous, yet overwhelming.

"Hello," says Susan Forks behind him.

Blount turns with a quiver, imagining that he has heard the voice of Yancey's granddaughter. Indeed he may; his senses have not deserted him, neither have his perceptions. It is indeed Susan standing inside the open door of his room, feet planted casually, little hands clasped before her. She must have been here for quite a while; Blount locked deep into his concentrative fit. How much of his Priestly dialogue has she overheard? Exactly how much of his life has he divulged?

Her eyes convey no message, neither does her posture. She breaks it loosely, turning to close the door firmly and hits the lock with precision. She drops the small handbag she had been carrying on the floor. She comes toward Blount slowly; he thinks he hears the music.

"I found out your room," she says quietly. "So I just came here and in. I wanted to talk to you."

Stay away from me! Blount wants to scream but he has always counteracted hysteria, in his life and out of it. Delicate as she is, Susan looks imposing from this angle, looming over him as he backs into a wall. She really cannot be any taller than he but she portrays an aspect of dimension while Blount has never felt so tiny.

"How long have you been here?"

"I just came in."

"Did you?"

"Of course I did," Susan says. "I don't eavesdrop on people." She looks at the Priest with interest. "What is that?"

"It's a confession machine from 1993. I got it very cheap."

"I've heard of them. Does it work?"

"What does it matter? Do you have anything to confess?"

"I was just curious," Susan says. She taps the machine; finding a hollow area of which Blount himself has never been aware. "I have nothing to confess, no."

"Then why bother asking if it works?"

"I don't want to argue. I didn't come here to argue with you Leslie." The *Leslie* hangs in the air like a bubble: dark, shocking. "He's supposed to get discharged tomorrow morning, that's what I wanted to talk about."

"I know he's supposed to be discharged tomorrow morning. I was the one who had to approve it."

"So?"

"So what?" Blount says. He is completely disoriented. Confusion, unhappiness run through him in a darkening line. He has never felt so unwell in exactly this way. "So I have to get back to my patient."

"He's being discharged tomorrow morning. Doesn't that mean anything to you?"

"I know what you mean," Blount says forthrightly, "and I haven't made up my mind yet. That's all."

"Made up your mind about what?" she says coyly. Dimples seem to float in her cheeks like seaweed on the surface of a still pond. She pats her shoulders, comes nearer to him. "I don't know what you're talking about."

"Don't you?" Blount says, but coyness has never been his strength despite his diminutive aspect, and his control oozes open. "I haven't decided what I'm going to do about him yet," he says. "And I'll make that decision alone."

"Oh," she says, "alone," closing the distance between them and Blount suspects, no he does not suspect but feels her shoulder prod against his rib-cage, small and hard, a point to put the pressure on; the contact seems to have a hint of oozing in it and he feels momentarily that they are sticking together but she does not draw away nor does little Blount. Something must be on his mind. "You've always been alone, haven't you?" she says.

"Most of us are."

"Having a thing like that in your room. That's a sad thing. I bet that you really talk to it don't you?"

"Now and then."

"And tell it all kinds of secrets that you've never told anyone else."

"I used to talk to my father a lot."

"But that wouldn't be the same thing. Not the same thing as another person." Her handbag drops to the floor with a clatter; he feels the pressure of her body fully against his from nape of neck to buttocks. "He's beginning to get strong again," she says. "The old man. They're going to discharge him and soon he'll be the same as he always was."

"That's the job here. To restore them. To get them back on their feet."

"And when he's the same as he always was, I'll be the same too."

She turns toward him at last, places her hands on his shoulders, puts her face against his neck. "You want me," she says, "I can tell that. Do you want me?"

"No."

"Of course you do. You've just been telling your confession machine over there in the corner how much you want me. I have ways of knowing."

"No such thing—"

"You can have me," she says. "Wait." She disengages from him, goes over to the door, checks the coils of the lock with small, sparing motions, then comes back to Blount again and stands before him, her hands moving up and down the ridges of her body. A good-looking girl; Blount can understand this objectively at least, the cheekbones giving the face more sensitivity than she may really have, the vigorous thrust of her breasts in outline rendering promise that she may never fulfill . . . but for all of that imminent cheat, the promise is there.

"Do you want me to undress?" she says. "I will, you know. I'll do anything you want."

"You don't understand," Blount says, "you never understood. I'm impotent. Neutered. All of us are. The process does this to us; the Projector destroys everything. This is part of the price of being a Messenger. Why do you think they recruit from Downside?"

"Nonsense," she says. "It's all a state of mind." She puts a hand on his elbow, guides herself against him again, tight in the joining. "Anyway," she says, "anyway, there are all kinds of ways of doing it. I know that you can feel. Everybody can feel something. Let me show you."

"No," Blount says. He tries to draw away from her but it does not work. "I told you, I can't feel. And it won't change what I'm going to do. What I do I do; it has nothing to do with you at all."

She smiles at him, a smile which could devour the

world and all of the Messengers in it as easily as the Projector devours dimension. "You fool," she says, putting her hands underneath her clothing and moving it up, up: he sees her breast. "You couldn't imagine that anyone could want you, could you? You couldn't see yourself taken for yourself."

"I see nothing."

She takes her robe off. He sees her bare to the waist, little glinting panels of flesh and behind it the emptiness. "Let me show you," she says. "Let me show you." She closes ground.

Blount stumbles back, feeling the floor shift beneath him, an elbow slamming painfully into the Priest. Groaning with pain he moves away from the machine which seems to look at him implacably; the angle of his flight from this carries him directly into Susan's arms. He feels her skin coming at him from all directions, feels himself at the verge of some intricate absorption and struggling, struggling, finds that it has been turned against him and that somehow he is swaddled in her arms moaning, his little mouth instinctively seeking her breast. "Yes," she says, "yes, that's what you want, that's what you need, that's what you always wanted." Immersed in the sounds of therapy Blount applies his tiny mouth and sucks and sucks; it is mildly pleasant, not altogether diverting but in general sequence and reaction the sensations at the emotional level—which he files away for further analysis at some other time—are complex and interesting.

Physically, of course, Blount feels nothing.

Well, that is all to the good; he has, after all, never felt anything; not even during his vigorous youth in Downside, jumping from building to building, dodging the incendiaries on the paths and generally preparing himself for acceptance of his father's systems theory of the universe. Not even then, certainly not now; this may be one of the reasons why he was led by his father so unprotestingly to the recruiting station. There is, to be sure, general awareness at least in Downside of what the Projector does to one, the reason why so many handsome little youths can be taken into the stations only in a state of unconsciousness or inebriation, but it did not bother Blount: in some fundamental sense he had nothing to lose, everything to gain. He has sucked a breast or two in his life. Blount has, has penetrated a cunt here and there with his throbbing little organ (although never since he entered the Institute) and at no time has Blount felt anything at all except a kind of sweatiness and the desire to end the accommodation as quickly as possible. He was able to function in the time before the Projector or so he thinks anyway, but the functioning had never given him any delight. Or, for that matter, pain. The word for this is narcosynthesia. He thinks. He will have to look it up some time.

In any event he sucks and sucks on Susan's left breast, properly curled in a nursing position, perched on his delicate knees on the floor while she smooths the back of his neck and looks on Blount with an expression both reflexive and tolerant. Is she getting anything out of this? Blount wonders idly; well he supposes she is; her breathing has become irregular. Then again it may only be (her eyes are closed as well) from contemplation of the murder of her grandfather which she will gain by this happy cooperation. No way of knowing. Hard to tell. Some of them are supposed to be very responsive there, Blount thinks. Then again, others are not.

Like Messengers, in fact. Some Messengers react to the Projector with horror, others with glee; some with anguish and all with uncertainty. But frightened or joyous, accepting or resisting, all of them are swallowed by the Projector and flicker to an eightieth of an inch in the same time in the same way. Emotions make no difference. Similarly, he thinks keenly, perhaps all of them close their eyes and breathe rapidly when they have their breasts sucked, whether they like it or not. Whether the sucker is excited or not. Whether the sucker feels rising in his joint or not and Blount does distinctly not, nothing is happening there at all (would he be amazed and frightened if it did?) and no way to get around this because through small gestures of her fingers, seizing his now and dancing around her hole, she is showing him that he is on the trail now of bigger outcome. He feels a hint of moisture on his fingers, little gusts seem to come from her cunt as if driven by a bellows.

"Come on," she says, "get inside now." Her speech is quite ragged. Her eyes open as if in death, lock on the ceiling. "Get it in, damn it, get it in!"

Get it in. No way to explain now that he would need a shovel and pick merely to wedge the hapless, useless organ in. No way to explain to her that she has got him all wrong; that her senses are now abusing her powers of common thought. No way, no way: she would surely know this herself or shortly will except that she is in no condition for conversation or advisements now, collapsing full-length to the floor, lying crosswise to the Priest now as if it were an altar and drawing up her knees to face the ceiling.

"For God's sake!" she says, "for God's sake, put that damned thing in or you'll kill me!"

Kill me.

Kill her . . .

Kill Yancey . . .

Everything is filled with death; even the act of generation seems to be drenched by its symbology. Blount whisks off his clothing; his little robes come off in a swoop, then his stockings, then his shoes, then his jewelry and appendages. Gladly would he discard his arms and legs and lie atop her like an hourglass, casting his brown sands first one way, then the other, but certain parts are permanently attached to him, no less than the pain. Naked then he confronts, falls atop her. He can try at least. He can try.

He always tried, Blount did: grant him this concession. He tried a little of this and then he tried a little of that; cheating and confession, love and submission, Priests and whores, Projectors and terminal patients; his range may have been narrow but it had depth. Only after everything else failed did he think of murder and then only with the greatest reluctance. With the greatest reluctance, folks: Blount does not think much, in general terms, of murdering and murderers. The act is too tentative for him, a displacement, a doubt: suicide would be better although strictly speaking Blount is not suicidal either. But give him credit. Give the little guy some applause, friends. Five feet one and full of fun, the evil he has performed in his life has always come with reluctance.

His blending with Susan Forks also occurs with reluctance: it is something to see how he twists and struggles atop her or then again maybe it is nothing to see, maybe it would be best to pass up the whole thing although this cannot be done. The camera is locked to position, it is full of film, and there is no leaving the premises until the shooting is completed although Blount, poor little Messenger, will not be shooting today. Still he is trying. Observe the face as the omnipresent camera snakes in; it is knotted with concentration, beaded with sweat, as firm and solemn as a death-mask as he pounds away, teeth gritted, below. His prick, coiled within itself, feels like a block of ice, still, however purposelessly, he flails to make enjambment. More comfort at her breasts; he would bend to suck at them again but she is holding him too tightly in this position and although his delicately chiseled chin is at their level, he simply cannot move the necessary inches to take them in his mouth. He is paralyzed. He is held against her and utterly trapped. Oh my, oh my, is Susan Forks a strong girl!

And, oh my, is she holding him! Blount feels locked in frieze forever; arms like iron gates clenched around his back, hands meeting in the center, pressing and drawing him in, mouth parted open, lips sawing away at his cheek.

"Come on," she says, "I know you want to do it; you *can* do it if you only concentrate, make it, make it!"

A girl, this one, educated to the belief obviously that intention can always flower toward achievement given time. No Downsider, she.

"Come *on*," she says, "*make* it!" and how can Blount explain? explanations are really beside the point and besides he does not want to disappoint her. He dives where Yancey dove, swoops where Yancey swept, dreams the dreams of Yancey as he bangs away at her, his joint like a little sausage in some vanished place and finally the motions slow, her energy decreases like some massive force of entropy being driven out of the universe, the universe dwindling and collapsing then and he feels her hands part, her arms drop away, her lips move to one side.

"My God," she says, "it's all true. I didn't believe it but it's true."

"I'm sorry," Blount says, the most purposeless comment of any he could make at this time but he *is* sorry; indeed a bright wire of shame heats within his body, he feels his disgrace spreading under the skin like a scar, will not abandon the hip-to-hip-lock in fact, so entrapped is he in remorse. "I wanted to, I really did, but I told you—"

"Get off me," she says, patting her hair back, terribly calm underneath him; he might be a dead mirror into which she is looking as she arranges her appearance. "Get off right now."

"I am," Blount says, his limbs are like stone but willing them to move he feels a twitch of response, forces that response into motion, thumps and clanks on the floor, his medallions jangling. "Don't you see—"

"What's wrong with you?"

"I told you," Blount says, thinking for some reason of the utter obtuseness of women. What is there about them? Unlike men (even Yancey) they cannot seem to accept visible evidences; they are very metaphysical . . . but unsystematized. "You were warned—"

"Don't you touch me!" she says, seizing her clothing like a large towel and waving it in his face. "Don't you just touch me—"

"I wasn't thinking of it. I was—"

"You tried to rape me!" she says, breathing unevenly, looking at the ceiling as she slips on her clothing. "Of course I resisted you, but you had your way anyway except that you couldn't do anything. Your sick mind, tormented by lust, was failed by your body. I'm going to tell them that."

"It's pointless," Blount says. "Don't you think everybody in the Institute, at least, knows about Messengers? I couldn't touch you."

"I'll tell them," she says, working her robes into place. "Unless you cooperate with me. My grandfather is a multimillionaire. I have money of my own. I can make your life miserable."

"What do you want me to do?"

"What do you think I want you to do?"

The coyness at least is gone; if Blount's failure has done nothing else it has taken off one mask. Of course it has only replaced it with another; Susan's rage is as compliant, as contrived as her flirtatiousness. Empty, empty thinks Blount and could weep. He will not weep, however. He never did a single thing. In his entire life, of it that life this truth will hold: Blount has done nothing. He has complied, he has accepted the dictates of superiors, he has moved through tunnels of purpose mined out through captured land. Everything has been borrowed. If he kills Yancey it will be the first thing in his life which Blount may say he has truly accomplished on his own.

"You disgust me," Susan is saying meanwhile. Quiet throughout the misguided and unfortunate attempt at sex she has recovered her sensibility and is talking, talking inexhaustibly. "You really do."

"It isn't my fault."

"I had heard things about the Messengers but I never knew—"

"Then whose fault is it?" Blount says quietly. Dressed himself now he walks to the door, unlocks and opens. The knob comes eagerly into his hand with a sensation of grease, never has the door opened so quickly. He shows Susan the empty hall, safe now for her perilous exit. "If you didn't listen, where may the fault be ascribed?" He feels grandiloquent; in fact he feels like a Priest. "Go," he says. His genitals give him no pain, they whisk under his robes harmlessly, moving in the direction of her intended exit. "It's safe, just go."

"Fault? Ascribed? Don't you talk to me."

"You started," Blount says. Strange, this: he feels soaring self-possession. He feels in command of himself. Having bottomed at last and having found that it is as bad (but no worse) than he ever conceived, Blount has nowhere else to go. "I didn't want to say a word to you."

"Sick," Susan says, pausing at the door. At the moment of flight, it seems, she cannot go. Blount has sympathy; he knows the feeling. "All of you are sick."

"Agreed."

"You shouldn't be allowed to exist. You shouldn't—"

"But we don't exist," Blount says reasonably. He closes the door on her, locks and bolts it. No sound from the hall, the walls of the Messenger's rooms are soundproof. Quite right: for the protection of the patients they must be bulkheaded in this way for most of the screaming comes from the inside.

"Don't exist," he repeats against the panels. The exaltation leaves him. It hisses out as did sex from Susan not so many moments ago. Alone in his room, he stands at odds with everything, strangeness coming over him. He feels that he has never seen this before in the way that he is now: the smooth blank pane of the bed, the rotting structure of the Priest, one window looking out on nothing, the closet door secured against his few possessions. How did he get here? What was on his mind? How did the wee fellow ever get to a place like this?

Really can't take it anymore, he mumbles. He stumbles to the Priest. His groin aches. Everything aches now; he feels pain like fumes coming from his belly. He is due back at Yancey's bedpost in less than an hour, his last night's vigil with the patient before release. How; how indeed is he going to go through with this? He is not sure. He is not sure of anything. Certainty has been squeezed from him through the wound of his sensation; now indeed Blount is convinced of nothing.

Humbly he goes to the Priest. The Priest has witnessed everything; if it will not speak it is, at the least, a repository. He kneels before it. The posture of the penitent feels easeful to him; it should, it is the posture of intercourse. But he knows that this time he will be the more successful.

"Free me, free me . . . for I have sinned," he says to the machine.

17

Blount imagines himself granted an appointment with Hulm. Ninety-four years old, deep into senile dementia caused by the stroke which has riven his brain; still the old man will see him; what a testament this is! What a tribute to Hulm's compassion, his vision, his involvement with the humble Messengers. But is this not truly written as part of the Founder's original notes on the device: *the Messenger is the key to all of this; it will take a very unusual man to bear those burdens but his vow will be to greatness.*

Blount always knew that if he should hit a monumental crisis he would be able to count upon Hulm himself. Now he is led humbly through halls and corridors, archways and openings, deep into the great mansion in which the Founder has lived, isolated from the world, for sixteen years by a hushed group of attendants, none of them over five feet three themselves, who check Blount at every stage of the journey for concealed weaponry and then pass him to the next level.

"He is a fine old man but in very poor contact; please limit your remarks," one of the attendants says to him on the way in; Blount says that he will, he only wants to ask the Founder a single question, that is all, and then will be on his way. Not for anything would he impose excessively on the time of the wonderful old man who singlehandedly opened the doorway for a new era of humanity.

At last, at last, he is taken into the bedroom of the great Hulm himself. There he is then, lying like a jewel on the bed, arms to his sides, blank eyes scanning the ceiling, ninety-four years and seventy-five pounds of courage and compassion, waiting to serve one of his youngest and most promising Messengers.

Blount gasps with the wonder of it, then prowls slowly near the bed and works himself into a deep knee-bend to draw his mouth close to the ears of the Founder and whisper his request to him. There are no other furnishings in the room; behind him a door slams and a key is turned. He understands that at last he is alone with the great old man and fears that his speech will be cut off by emotion but no: he has misjudged himself again, he feels lucid and in control of himself.

"Hello, Founder," he whispers to the rigid old man. "I have a problem about which I must have counsel from you alone."

Hulm waves a hand as if to indicate that Blount may speed right along. Of course the distinguished and deeply fulfilled old Founder has not said a word for nineteen years but all the reports say that his mind is as alert and full-ranging as ever; his failure to speak is less the hemispheric damage of the stroke (which could be overcome) but a *willingness not to speak;* a message there for all the generations of Messengers and his disciples that words mean nothing. Still Blount feels just a shade disappointed; it would be a sensational thing if he could get the old man to say something after all these years. Well, he can try.

"What I'm thinking about doing is committing a murder of a patient," Blount goes on. "A patient under my care that is; an old man, the name isn't important, not as old as you are but getting right along there, eighty-three years old now, something like that. He seems to think that I'm corrupt and frankly I don't like his attitude if you follow what I'm saying. I mean: who the hell is he to say that I'm corrupt when I'm the one who saved him? Do you see what I mean? And there are other things too.

All in all, I'm really just on the verge of committing a murder."

The Founder waves his arm again; a thin string of wire against the sheets. His eyes blink, he stirs on the bed; something seems to have excited him. In fact his withered hands beat now against the sheets like an insect; Blount is afraid that he may be starting a fit of some kind. How embarrassing. What would Blount do? Without the old man to confirm that his words were harmless, the impression might get around that Blount had made some kind of attack or had otherwise excited the old fellow beyond his ability to deal with the situation. It certainly would not bode well for his future.

"Hey!" he says. "Calm down. It's nothing certain yet. I mean I haven't actually done it and for all I know I'm not going to do it. Certainly not without your permission. All that I need is the opportunity to talk things out a bit so that I can get it straight in my head. You don't think that I'm an actual murderer, do you? I mean, someone who wants to commit murder isn't necessarily a murderer if you can make the distinction; I haven't made a *habit* of thinking this way and whatever else happens I promise that I'll never get into a situation like this again. It's just a sort of passing phase. Isn't it? You don't have to look at me that way; I never had an evil thought in my life. I didn't ask for Yancey, he was assigned to me. It could have been anyone. Stop looking at me that way, damn it!"

Oh indeed Blount is upset; Blount is indeed having what may be diagnosed as a paranoid episode of one sort or the other. It is not so much that the Founder is looking at him from some deep posture on the bed, many people have looked at the wee fellow in his time and not all of the glances have been unfriendly, but the stare of the Founder in collaboration with the continuing tapping of the hands on the sheets, the feeling of closure which seems to spread from the confrontation quite upsets him. Also, the Founder is now having some kind of a coughing fit. It must be coughing; certainly it is not speech, speech would not sound this way: hacks and groans filtering from his mouth, much gentle spraying of sputum, tremors and flutters in the neck which take and shake the Founder so that he moves spiritlessly in the bed like a large shrunken fish.

"Come now," Blount says, "it's not that bad, is it? You must have understood that someday in some way at least one of your Messengers would want to kill." But the Founder is simply not to be comforted; tears now pour down his cheeks and as if being dangled in suspension from the ceiling he seems to dance in the bed.

Blount casts frantic glances toward the door; perhaps someone will come in to help him; but the door remains closed and the walls, of course, are impenetrable. The Founder of the Institute, the immortal and time-honored Hulm himself is having a final attack of some kind in his bed and Blount the only witness; when they come in at last to announce the interview over they will find the precious old sage lying dead and what will they do to Blount then? Blount is already in deep trouble with the Yancey matter to say nothing of the involvement with the granddaughter (Messengers are never supposed to become involved with relatives); this will finish him off.

He looks toward the door, decides that he must make the best of a bad situation and flee. Down the hall he can explain what is going on here or then again he cannot; he may, if luck is with him, simply walk out of the Founder's home and out the gate without apprehension. Let them discover Hulm then. Let them try to pin it on Blount. He will make use of the services of the best lawyer he can find. His salary, even in escrow, will support it.

No such events. The door is locked, the handle spins uselessly in his hand. He should have realized that they would lock him in with the Founder precisely for this reason. Hulm's cunning may, in fact, have led to this situation: perhaps he has typed out advisements that his door is to be kept locked during interviews so that potential assassins will be trapped. Why not?

Blount comes back from the door, ponders the old man on the bed. The tremors, to some degree, have subsided, but something worse is happening; clearly Hulm is making some desperate attempt now to speak. Little bubbles of words break free from the side of his mouth, hang in the open air.

Goma, the Founder says. *Ah blewshite. Witches.* Something is clearly happening but Blount cannot comprehend the words. He does not speak the language.

Slowly he puts his hands on the old man's wrists and presses him back on the bed. Soothingly, calmly, he passes skillful palms over the sweating forehead; he must keep the old man calm. That is his only thought; to somehow preserve the situation in stasis until more sensible hands come in to rescue him.

"Stop it!" he pleads. "I didn't mean it; I mean if that's what is upsetting you, you just put it right out of your mind because I wouldn't hurt a flea. Not a flea or a patient; you know me, five feet one, on the run and full of fun, just a little bit of a kidder. You get a pretty crude sense of humor being brought up in the Downsides; you ought to know that too you wonderful old man, how could you take me seriously? Blount won't kill. Blount kills no one."

Strange how the paper of the old man's flesh feels and even looks like Yancey's against the sheets. In fact, the profile of the Founder, as he shakes his head and points it toward the wall is also very similar to Yancey's; amazing how Blount did not see this until the moment. Well, he has had a lot on his mind lately. Say that he is on edge.

Still, it is astonishing, he thinks, as he pins the helpless wrists against the sheets and looks at the beating and fluttering of Hulm's eyes; he looks exactly like Yancey although a little older. What is imminent in Yancey has been accomplished with the Founder; the old man has collapsed, his systems, such as they are, would no longer be self-maintaining but surely Yancey, operation or not, is headed on the same road . . . if he lives. It would be even easier to kill the Founder than Yancey, come to think of it; ninety-four versus eighty-three: oh, nothing to it at all!

Killing corpses appears to be Blount's sub-specialty, or at least thinking of killing them. He considers the Founder carefully. Now that it is all falling into alignment and he is starting to think clearly for the first time since he met Yancey, it would indeed be easy to kill the Founder. In fact, it would no doubt be a service.

Why not? It would relieve a burdened staff of unhappy duties; it would relieve Hulm himself of the weight of his mortality, his desiccation, his collapsing support systems. Surely if the fine old man were in possession of his faculties, he would not want to live on in this way. *Better off dead,* he imagines Hulm whimpering under his wrists, the words moving the wasted body like a pendulum. *Yes sir, lad, you don't know how long, long I've waited. Do it fast: do it with the hands or knife but get it over with; you don't know the prayers, the dreams, the longing for release and now at last you're here; 'tis a dream, lad, a dream . . .*

Clearly that is what Hulm would say; how could he not say it? How could he take any other position on his future granted the circumstances. Oh, Blount thinks that he can hear the whispering, it is very close. He is maddened by need, the little Messenger is; never has he felt so close to his purposes as in this perilous proximity to Hulm. He has journeyed a thousand miles and now, at last, his terrible quest is over. He can do the Founder a favor. Also, he can straighten out his own life.

Slowly, he increases the pressure on the old man's wrists. *That's it son* the voice seems to be saying, *you're on the right track* and he squeezes harder, now harder indeed. He could crack Hulm like kindling in the bed. He moves over the Founder, chest to chest, coming astride him and gently moves his skillful fingers toward the old man's windpipe. So easy. It was always so easy. He has struggled and struggled for insight and all the time, always, it lay underneath him in a bed in a mansion a thousand miles away; now at last, all resolution clear, he bends his face toward that of the Founder.

"I want you to understand," he says quite reasonably, "that there's nothing personal in this for me at all. I take no satisfaction from it whatsoever. I'm simply here to do you a favor."

A favor. A service. No emotion. No closeness, no satisfaction. Messengers are supposed to take no emotional satisfaction from their work; they are warned against this, as a matter of fact, in the classroom. Once the Messenger begins to find his duties actually pleasant he risks losing control of his skills. This is not to say, of course, that he should hate his work. No one ever asked a Messenger to *hate* the work. Emotional detachment, yes. That is all. A task like many to be performed. In and out of the body's cavity, hack up the body like a slab of meat. Of course. That is all. Nothing else whatsoever.

Blount reminds himself that he is not to enjoy what he is doing. Murdering the Founder is a serious business; it must be taken on that level. He is taking it on that level. The old man's breath is sealed off like placing a cork in a bottle; Hulm begins to inflate with his own gases. Closer and closer. There cannot be much strength left in a ninety-four-year-old body. Blount applies himself to the task, the emotional edges retracting further. Harder and harder. In and out. Hulm flops in the bed. His body dilates. His eyes open and look into Blount's. In those eyes; Blount sees his own face. He feels no horror. He looks no different than he has in years. Murder is not changing his features nor deforming them with complexity. It is now, it is always to be, it has always been the same old Blount.

Under him the old man turns into Yancey. It is no longer the Founder in the bed but Yancey. Yancey lays underneath him with open eyes penetrating Blount's, his fingers draping over Blount's shoulders like a lover's, his body, in its last struggles, heaving toward his Messenger's in an embrace. All right. Fine. He should have suspected that at the last moment something like this would be arranged. The Founder is cunning, the men who surround to protect him are cunning; certainly they would not yield up his life so easily. Early in the courses they were taught of the infallibility of Hulm.

You may trust the Projector, you must trust the Projector, the equations are firm and reliable.

The man who created those equations was not liable to error. The Projector will reduce you to operative size, its effects will wear off, you will return to normal dimensions. Never has the process failed. Those Messengers who have gone insane during or after stress misunderstood the infallibility of Hulm. Trust Hulm. Trust the Founder always. He will not fail. Nothing will fail.

Underneath him, Yancey croaks like a frog. Thinking of these things Blount has relaxed his grip; the old bastard, still strong, has managed to berathe. With the intake of breath comes vitality, with the vitality, motion. Yancey moves in the bed, leaps in the bed, arches in the bed like a fish. Frenzy gives him the strength to sit upright, tossing Blount in a heap to the floor. Stunned, the Messenger cannot find his balance for a moment; in that time Yancey has hit the call bell beside his bed frantically, three times, four times, six times. Now, there are scurryings in the hallways.

Scurryings in the hallways, thumps on the door. They are coming to get him. They will apprehend and jail him for attempted murder. Blount knows that he must arrange some kind of escape but he cannot get his limbs to move. He wills motion but nothing happens; he scrapes on the floor like a skater. The door opens. Attendants come in. There are many of them, more than those who escorted him into this room. They look from Blount to the bed. Yancey has turned into Hulm again. The traitorous bastard will not hold onto an identity; it is the Founder who lies there, arms crossed over his chest, looking at the ceiling. He looks peaceful. He looks dead.

Blount does not know what to say. He is somewhat at a loss for words. He opens his palms and spreads his arms, pleading for some sort of understanding. "Surely you should have some compassion for me gentlemen," the little fellow says as attendants close in upon him. "You more than anyone should know what a Messenger has to contend with these days." No, this does not seem to be the right approach. The attendants are displeased. Their expressions are ferocious.

"You killed the Founder," one of them says, making a chopping motion with his hand against thigh. "Now we're going to have to kill you."

Blount checks the bed. Yes, it is Hulm again lying in state, death-mask propped to the ready. Yancey seems to have deserted the fortress. All of the time, then, they were aligned to get him. "Listen here," he says, "that's not fair."

"What isn't fair?"

"Well, saying you'll kill me because I killed the Founder. Now, not admitting for a moment that I *did*," Blount says hastily as the attendants seize him, "because we all love him as you know and such a thing is *inconceivable*, but just for the sake of the discussion, it would be very unfair of you to kill me just because I killed the Founder because after all he was ninety-four years old and in very poor condition whereas I'm twenty-two. Only twenty-two years old, gentlemen, and I have years of *useful life* ahead of me."

This is not working either. No; it was definitely an error to adopt this line of discussion. Blount wishes that he had never started.

"I didn't do it," he says.

The attendants twist his arm.

"I didn't mean to do it anyway," he concedes.

Attendants break his arm, rather painlessly.

"Anyway, if I meant to do it it was for a higher purpose," he adds.

His ankle is twisted; he feels a kneecap shearing.

"Okay," he concludes, "I had to do it and I meant to do it all the time but it's a pretty lousy job being a Messenger as you can well imagine and all of this regret and loathing has to come out somewhere."

The attendants nod. This at least has penetrated; Blount is speaking to them at last on a common level of discourse. "Of course," they say in *unis* and *a capella*, "you have an excellent point there but it's still your life and you've got to accept the responsibility for it. It hasn't been easy for you but a great number of people get into circumstances not of their own choosing and make the best of it and you must too Blount. It is your life, it is your destiny, nothing must intervene."

They fall atop him. They lift him like a bell above their heads. Everything happens swiftly; they slam him into a wall and with a great relieving clap Blount passes out of the Founder's mansion, out of his speculations, and back to the simple level of his perceptions where he finds himself lying sprawled beside the Priest in the deepness of the dark, one hand outstretched to clutch the old Priest, the other pounding away on the floor. Apparently, he has been dreaming.

He stands. Blount stands in the room. Surfaces waver around him, then reorder themselves as is customary after brief disorientation. It is very much like coming to full size from the Projector, everything restores itself then too quickly for nausea. Blount releases his saving grip on the Priest and looks around his room. He is late for shift. It is time to be with Yancey.

Only time for one more thing; he must make it this time no matter what happens. He touches the Priest, then falls before it, pressing in his forehead, meditating. He opens his mouth. He speaks.

"Forgive me Father for I am about to sin," Blount says.

18

And comes at last to do the deed. Blount looks upon the sleeping Yancey. The old man lies still in the bed, even dreams, even pulse, no soporifics but the natural rest of the conscienceless. He has recovered and in hours he is going home. It his last night.

Blount looks upon the old man, standing isolated against the wall; he looks at his own hands, the skillful, now trembling hands of Blount which are extended before him, sculpting graceless little arcs before him in the empty air.

With these hands I thee kill the wee fellow thinks but this seems overly dramatic and posturing. It does not suit the occasion at all. It does not suit old Yancey. Something a little more straightforward, if you will.

"I have no choice," he says instead; "No choice at all you see; I've simply got to do it. Don't ask me why."

Yancey makes no comment. He lies dumb on the bed, swaddled by the vapors of his own breath. His rest is total; he neither thinks nor does he commune. Eighty-three, he is still a mystery. Now in sleep his past is as unknown as his future. He could be anyone. He could be anyone at all.

Blount shrugs, bolts the door. He has been bolting his share of doors lately or having them bolted for him; more and more he seems to live in a series of enclosures. Not his fault; just the way it evolved, folks. Creature of circumstance, Blount, from the very beginning: *why I never had an original idea in my life!* the elf thinks. He twirls the knob in his hands. Impermeable. To be sure he slides a chair subtly against the door, pins it to place. Good. Good enough. No one is going to get into this room without either Blount's explicit permission or the use of incendiaries. Certainly the window may be considered secure.

Musing, Blount moves back to the bed. He decides to switch on the lights in the room to better contemplate his target; if the sudden flash awakens Yancey, so be it. He will glimpse Blount's purposes in an instant and hold himself trembling and this is acceptable. He can kill Yancey as easily in knowledge as disbelief; then out of his hands. Let Yancey do as he will. The lights pop; Yancey shows no reaction whatsoever. He is really quite comfortable, make no mistake about it. Rubbing his hands together, Blount, the assassin, closes in.

"I want you to know why I have to do this," he says very quietly, not to awaken the patient if he can help it, but informed as always with the reasonable need for explanation. "It isn't because of the things you said to me and it isn't because of your damned granddaughter either, although she could have driven me to it if I was on the line. I admit that. It's just because it has to be done. You've got to be put out of your misery. I can't take this anymore. *You* can't take it anymore. What I giveth, I also have the right to taketh away; that seems perfectly fair, doesn't it?"

It does not, in fact. It sounds querulous, almost as if Blount were whining. He does not want the invisible audience (who is leaning forward keenly in their seats now; at last folks, at last a hint of real action!) to think that he is committing this dreadful act from an abscess of self-pity. This was not the way it was ever intended. Instead, Blount wanted to kill from the purest, highest, finest motives of all: he wanted to better himself. Not from shame but for achievement's sake.

"Perfectly reasonable," little Blount murmurs, circling in upon the sleeping, shaking form, now as depersonalized as a piece of furniture. "It was perfectly reasonable from the beginning. *I* was perfectly reasonable from the beginning. It could have been no other way."

Bits of history, hints of rumor circulate through his bloodstream as he closes the gap. He remembers awful tales told behind doors in the Institute; stories that at the beginning an inordinate number of patients were dying from inexplicable causes, far beyond the Founder's projected mortality rate. Patients were found dead in their beds at noon, patients were stricken by embolism days after discharge, patients incurred hemispheric damage in the halls of the Institute while shambling back and forth on practice runs: what exactly was happening? The Projector was a blessing, it was recognized from the outset that the process was not so much in need of sale as selection, but there were certainly a great number of accidents occurring and if the situation was not controlled it would certainly put a considerable dent in business which at the time was building mightily.

So there had been quiet but profound investigations in which the Founder himself had taken a hand (the rumors continued; those were long bleak nights in training and very little for the troops to do; the staff had tried to discourage them from speculating too freely or associating with one another intimately but the trainees knew exactly where the staff could go in this regard) and after a time certain facts had shuffled themselves into light like an itinerant magician, slowly but successfully extracting the proper cards from a deck; there was a correlation between certain frequencies of such accidents and Messengers on the various cases. At that time the individual responsibility of the Messenger for his patient had not been established; assignments rotated, one Messenger could treat several patients, one loose team of Messengers could work on a number of patients: it took subtle statistical research and patience to begin to make the connections but connections at last were made . . .

it appeared, there was no way around this, that given Messengers, not a majority but more than a few, were killing their patients . . . or at least failing to contribute to their living.

At this time, Blount thinks cleverly, switching on the Projector which comes to life with its usual low hum, little flashes of controlled light bouncing within the housing, at this point the Institute could have made any one of a number of decisions, adopted any one of a number of courses, but what they did in its profound clarity was probably, alongside the Projector, its greatest single contribution to its own success: it did not discharge the suspected Messengers or even bring them up for some kind of investigation—the publicity would have been ruinous; one breath of this hitting the public domain and that would have been the end of the process, who would pay fifty thousand dollars to get himself *killed?*—but instead gathered the information to itself like a lover . . . and killed the study.

The suspected Messengers were reassigned to positions cutting them off from direct contact with the patients. Their enlistments were continued. They were granted administrative duties. Some of them became instructors. Quite a few rose high in the organization and many of them were now heading up or near to heading up some of the Institutes.

So they had a good chance of being taught or supervised by an ex-Messenger who in his time had committed a couple of murders, before the Institute had gathered itself to the great insight that individual culpability (the assignment of one Messenger to one case from admission through discharge) could solve the problem through fear. They had a good chance of meeting at one time or another a cold, clinical murderer . . . but this need not concern the young trainees; the fact of murder had been built so deep into the Institute from the beginning—what was the Projector itself but a kind of deliberately invoked death?—that it could only serve to add a certain level of excitement to their conditioning.

The trainees filled their nights and leave-times with such speculations and reminiscences; it filled them up satisfactorily and there was, for most of them certainly, little enough to do otherwise. They were not going to spend their leave-times in Downside.

So Messengers had been murdering patients; this was part of the clear folklore of the Institute, and at least Blount, in his growing certainty, had never felt reason to argue the point. Now, watching the projector come to flame, the slow glow of its functioning leaping and burning inside, Blount finds himself thinking that he is not so much contemplating a crime as a return of myth. The reconstitution of myth. The reversion to necessity.

Yes indeed. He has thought about the best means of doing it and has decided upon the Projector. Projector reduction, that was the way; he would go inside Yancey and carefully sever the plumbing of the body. Anything simpler than this would not have been proper; he could murder the old bastard in his bed, of course; he could even pump the room full of gases and make a quiet exit; but nothing to Blount had the clear economy of ending the job in the way that he had begun. Also, also: there was at least a chance this way, using the Projector that is, that he would not be caught.

And all things being put together, Blount would just as soon not be caught. He has come to this decision recently; it is nothing personal of course, since he has always had the highest respect for those in authority and in fact would not quite know what to do with his life outside of an institutional framework . . . nevertheless, Blount can think of ways in which he would more usefully like to spend his declining years than in a prison of some sort. He may, after his term of enlistment is up, resign from the Institute and begin his memoirs; he may take another enlistment in order to accumulate enough money to enjoy a fruitful retirement. Or he may do none of these things whatsoever; simply dedicate these years to quiet and fruitful endeavors like trying to rewire the Priest and re-establish communication with it.

But the hearing, the trial, the dock, the judgment are not for Blount: Yancey is simply not worth it to the Messenger. He has judged the extent of his passion toward Yancey and it is minor, residing somewhere between his feelings about the Founder and his father, both of them far better off dead, to be sure, but not also of the most consuming personal interest. Essentially Blount wants to kill Yancey because he is an annoyance, an intrusion, in the same way, perhaps, that he would crush a nattering insect.

No, if there is any passion in this affair and Blount does not care to plumb it at the present time . . . but if passion is an element, it would only come in with the question of the granddaughter. Now *Susan,* Blount thinks, Susan he might be able to kill with pleasure and take the penalty. If he had an easy chance. But Yancey—

No, Yancey is a dream, a constituent of Blount's rather distorted view of the universe, not its cause. The old man now mumbles something in his sleep; he still does this quite a bit (apparently a light sleeper by heredity): "Fuck the sons of bitches," Yancey says quietly. "That's all I have to say. Fuck 'em, fuck 'em."

He turns over on his other side, faces the wall quite painlessly. Blount quite agrees with these thoughts. Fuck the sons of bitches indeed. But where, who, and how? This is the problem he has never quite been able to resolve.

Nevertheless, nevertheless: it is a creed for the holding, he supposes, as efficacious as any of the others. *Fuck the sons of bitches.* He thinks about this, running his little lance (the size of a mere pinpoint at this aspect but he has enormous manual skills) across his wrists to test the sharpness, then carefully replacing it in its pouch. Everything in order. Definitely, definitely the lance will work.

Everything else seems to be in place too. The Projector hums itself on a rapid whine, ascends to a high note (an A flat thinks Blount idly but he has no musical talent at all; he merely remembers his lessons), then quiets to stasis, rapidly whirring. He unseals its beam by opening a metal clip, a pure fork of light darts out and hits the opposite wall, only a few feet above Yancey's sleeping figure. It must be realigned; these things do happen. Sweatily, he must have run his hands over the Projector sometime recently and disoriented the thrust of the beam.

Blount hums fragments of his favorite *Glouscester Retrieval* to himself while setting the beam up properly. Why has no one ever thought of throwing the Projector on the *patient?* it would certainly simplify disposal problems and would be as painless a device as any other. The only problem would be that, crushed or not, discarded or not, stomped, dismembered, burnt or beaten, the corpse would, in separate pieces or as a totality, move with idiot energy to reconstitute itself after the suitable interval and one would be left with a very large, unpleasant means of disposal. If the corpse were to reconstitute itself while the Messenger were unfortunately proximate to the scene, he could be unpleasantly and embarrassingly injured, in fact.

And if not, if there were a way out of this, then some murder-inclined Messenger would surely have taken to swallowing his patients in the hall of the night. But reconstitution is reconstitution. According to the dicta of the great Hulm himself, no one can avoid it: not Messengers, not patients. What the Projector giveth the Projector doth savage back and one would drop its deadly little beam on the patient only at severe risk.

No. Far better to do it traditionally, then; Blount's inventive streaks have always been disastrous anyway. Think of the Priest. With a final nod and wink at the wall, then, the wee fellow settles himself before the Projector, carrying his pouch in extended hands before him, glinting in a palm, feels the forceful rays of the Projector hitting him and as always succumbs to a brief illusion of power as the beam wafts through him: he will grow, he will ascend mightily, he will achieve enormous size and control over the world.

Unfortunately the process works the other way. He has never been able to quite escape that initial feeling of shock. With some amount of spirit Blount dwindles; rapidly the world increases in size.

So does Yancey. The process all told cannot take more than thirty seconds; one of its great advantages is that all happens indeed so very quickly that there is little time to contemplate. Yancey, perceived from this angle as Blount hops upon the frozen sheet becomes enormous, filling his vision, a gigantic, bloated frame arching ceilingwards, taking on the outlines of an ancient dirigible, ponderous, overwhelming Blount, and still he is shrinking. Soon he can no longer define Yancey in human outline at all; shortly after that he has lost all sense of context and must proceed by other signs. Pores like craters loom before him on a field of white, he wishes that he could disappear into those pores and find entrance in that way. Easier, much easier folks, if the sheer scatology of the job could be cancelled. Still, what is there to do? What can the diminutive little chap do? He must make his entrance in the accustomed way.

Now he is one-eightieth of an inch tall. If he did not have his beam to guide him he might become hopelessly lost on a six-foot-long hospital bed, Blount might find himself charging around the outlines of that bed with the desperation that old explorers found themselves approaching the end of the flat world, shrieking for all he is worth.

Fortunately he is quite experienced; the true implications of what has happened to him are assimilated by Blount as quickly as that world outside. Yancey absorbs gulp after gulping breath. Blount removes the beam from his pouch, focuses it on what he takes to be a desirable area and turns it on to full as he whisks his way under the world. Trotting rapidly, at least thirty feet a minute if he can only keep the pace going, Blount finds the specter of a cavity which can only be Yancey's anal opening. Excellent. Everything is proceeding as if proper. This essay in murder is going along with the smoothness of a routine adventure: never, never, have the indications shown less foreboding. Blount works his way through the forest of hairs ringing the anal sphincter and easily, as if greased, dives all the way down.

The camera, as if modest (it is not modest but certain literary devices must apply even to Blount's life; some of the intrusive delicacy of the 80's, say, when it was discovered that euphemisms had greater worth and depth than explicit narrative to say nothing of the approval of the governmental censoring agencies) gives way to a slow, yellow dissolve; when it returns to our subject it finds him in a different attitude. Now he is a man in flight, running through the capillary walls as if pursued by ravening corpuscles (which he is, which he is; if a Messenger were to exceed his welcoming time in the body he would find himself in grim hand-to-hand combat, he would) or his devouring conscience, making tracks into the intestine, prodding away for purchase with his lance, stumbling and staggering but continuing to make that steady progress which has always been Blount's distinguishing highlight. He has never had the grace of most Messengers but through stubborness and a hold upon his balance he has always been able to make the moves. This has been his purchase out of Downside, it is already shaping the outlines of his future: it will be the skillful murder that Blount has become.

At length he finds himself in the sheath blocking off the small from the large intestine, easing himself through porous material at last to stand in a small enclosure which, lit by fibers and little arterial pulses as it is, has somewhat of the aspect of Blount's own familiar rooms. He feels at ease within this enclosure; he perches upon a strange mushroom-shaped object that makes a satisfactory seat. He fits his lance between his legs and adapts a contemplative posture.

Blood thunders like a waterfall around him but Blount is safe. He inhales the foul gusts of Yancey's air and finds it good. He is a man at ease. He has, to check by his timer, five minutes only in which to commit his dreadful deed and get out.

Five minutes is enough; Blount has already planned his modus operandi. A prick in the vulnerable area exposed by the removal of the tumor, an area weakened and strained by the parting of fibers, will cause a small but increasing hemhorrage deep within Yancey. Blood will strain, first in droplets through the tiny opening, then in pulses and finally in a clear, steady stream which will pour through both intestines, opening up everything through which it rushes, tearing and gashing with its increased speed and soon Yancey will be in serious trouble indeed: without a mark on his body, a change in his facial expression, a quiver in the cerebral hemisphere he will be losing literally quarts of blood through errant transfer from the right area of his body to the wrong one. His stomach will bulge, inflate with this blood, he will feel a whiplash in his bowels like a serpent diving from one barricade to the next for cover, he will seize his belly in sudden, comic fury and lurching from the bed stagger toward the latrine . . . but this one motion, this gigantic upheaval will set off the explosions within the body proper; Yancey will be given back to Yancey in the ruined blood and he will lie on the floor of the bathroom or just slightly out of it, moving like a frog, whistling the popular tunes of death while his life strains away from him in the large but still invisible leakage.

None of it will be difficult, all predictable: it should take no more than an hour from the incision of Blount's lance to the commencement of the last services over the corpse. Less if Yancey should move around more in his bed during the early hemhorraghic instances.

Blount smiles. He could indeed so immerse himself in consideration of Yancey's impending dilemma that he might neglect to actually do the deed itself but no chance; there can be no chance of it at all because a little clock is booming away in Blount's skull louder than his timer and this clock cannot fail; he will wait three minutes and begin the cutting. To do it immediately might be dangerous; Blount cannot leave the body too early because of the risks of being very, very small in a large world, he must remain therefore in the body as close to the time of restoration as possible . . . and so if he makes the cut too early he risks drowning in the patient's blood if the embolism is sudden or violent. Oh my he is cunning, Blount: cunning has stalketh him all of his days and now at last has thrown its small net of blessing upon him: he knows that he will not fail.

"Forgive me please for I believe that I am going to sin," he murmurs, surrounded by the waterfalls of blood.

"But I want you to know that I regard this really as an opportunity," he adds hastily.

No one, not even an unseen auditor or the audience pressing in upon the developing events, should think that Blount has any reservations whatsoever about his impending deed. To the contrary, he treasures it: he regards it as an opportunity. It will utterly free him. How many, even Messengers, have the opportunity to be absolutely free?

"I do believe," Blount says, noting his timer, "that I am definitely about to sin now if you will permit me to do that."

He rises. The technicolor of the body bedazzles him as he prepares his lance, then tiptoes into the abscess of his employment. There is centrifugal force in the body; he must watch his step very carefully now or one misstep could plunge him toward disaster, but old skill will serve him well now: Blount has never deserted skill, even in his darkest moments, and so it is not that skill will desert him now. He finds the proper place, the same way as he had left it four days ago, hanging empty and fibrous, a small pocket marking the point of exit of the tumor and stands before it briefly in awe, somewhat as a man might stand before a natural monument or a death-mask of another assassinated Chief of State: he has done this. It is his work, the work of Blount which he is regarding. No one will ever see it (unless Yancey's body after death is declared a state resource and autopsied), no one will ever know that it existed, but Blount's handicraft hangs before him now and it is something to behold.

In a way it is a shame to intervene with the destiny he has inflicted upon this body. Yancey might live ten or fifteen more years with Blount's patchwork. Still it is duty to be done here: nothing more nor less and implacably Blount moves forward now, holding his lance. A twitch of remorse holds him back; he ignores it. A shade of recrimination passes over his features like a darkening cast; he realigns those features and urges his way in. He extends the lance. It seems that the moment may be held in frieze eternal as the camera eases in on his troubled brow, his demented little eyes, then it swings back and what was fated to be becomes completely apparent. He bores in. Blount severs fibers. He applies the tiny flame to the end of the equipment and burning, burning, circles inward. Nerve matrixes part. Capillaries shriek their anguished little song. Blood vessels fling upward and pant in the deadening air. Blount saws away. His mouth fuses in a mad little whistle.

Shards and fragments of the *Gloucester Retrieval* bubble through his mind, competing with other Great Moments Of The Popular Song; it is hard to keep all of it properly sorted away in its various channels. *Left my love-a graven heart-making a refreshing start-Watch an old lady turning blue in the street-watch the stars hanging like meat-Feel like I'm living on a trampoline-lowdown spoiled wicked and mean-That's the Downside Blues-Oh Mister, please.* Popular song did not experience one of its periodic bursts of lyricism in the middle nineties, to be sure. Nevertheless, it is the only history that Blount has possessed: filled with junk as it may be it still remains the furnished room of his life and the attachment is severe.

Oh Mister, please-the Downside Blues. Oh Mister,

Yancey is gushing.

Blood is pouring from the abscesses of the old body as if a series of faucets have been opened. Blood leaps, sings, dances in the air, showers Blount with little traces, he dodges back and almost loses his balance, could fall into a vessel and drown. He had not judged this. Nothing this spectacular had ever occurred to him.

He must have not judged, that is all there is to it, the true precariousness of Yancey's condition; egotistical Blount, meglumaniacal Blount assumed that because he had settled one condition he did not have an eighty-three-year-old ruined body still on his hands, but Yancey has no ability to withstand the stress of the cuts inflicted. Blood is not pouring with the neat vigor which a healthy body would sustain but instead is roaring, foaming, bubbling along like a set of mad cesspools heading straight toward the body's sewers.

Ulp, Blount says uselessly. Really now, what else is there for him to say? he might conceive of a few poetic words, recriminations, powerful renunciations for Yancey, but the fact is that he is extremely nauseated by what he has wrought. It is a disgusting spectacle taking place here, no question about it, and Blount is really not geared: he had thought of something cleaner. His thoughts had been pure, spiritual, metaphysical; he had not predetermined the sheer *bloodiness* of the acts he was to perform.

Now he looks upon his handiwork and is sickened. *Ah God* the wee fellow says and leaps a little higher for tricky purchase upon a vein, *who would have believed it?* The venous tissue is weak; he feels the blood pulsing within. In an instant the vein itself could go dangerously askew, exploding blood like thunder and then where would he be? No, Blount understands, he has got to get out of here.

Terrible fear overtakes him. He has known fear all his life: fear of Downside, fear of the Projector, fear of the Priest, fear of Yancey's knowledge, but he has never known until right now all-out physical fear, literal fear for his life, and as it courses through him he comes to realize that all the rest of it was for nothing. *Angst* and spiritual despair definitely have their place in the scheme of life and are not to be derogated but for sheer bowel-loosening, disorienting, gasping terror there is nothing like an actual life-threat. Blount has, in the eddies and whorls of blood now lost sight of a clear escape-line; how is he going to get out of here? He sees the intestine hanging before him, ruddy, damp, busy meat but the intestine is swamped with blood and too slipped to scurry, the only other exit would be down the network of capillaries, a blind exit into the anus and any misstep or, for that matter, any total blowout—which looks imminent—will be the end of him.

"I didn't mean it!" the little fellow squeaks pitifully, holding his ground from fear. "I really didn't mean it; I'm terribly sorry."

A lot of good that is doing him now. A lot of good indeed . . . he hears the sound of the blood as it rips around and toward him like a waterfall and screams with horror. It is as if Yancey himself has leapt inside his own body and enormously, vengefully, has turned the network upon him. Blount cowers, slides across the vein, finds himself straddling it like a log. The purchase is perilous; it rocks and beats underneath him. Yancey feels as if he is going up.

And it is this, this alone which finally galvanizes Blount. Not anger, not courage, not even self-preservation but blind, squealing terror, the terror of the pig about to be slaughtered moves him from the vein. He sways first one way, then the other, holds, then lets go and falls into a rapidly moving red stream, gasping and flailing his little arms as the stream carries him along. Somewhere in this he loses his lance; it is torn from his fingers and vanishes forever and now the swimmer, encumbered only by his tight-fitting gear, devotes all of his efforts to merely holding on. He no longer knows where there is an exit or what he wants to do; he no longer has even a sense of identity. What sustains him is simply the need to breathe, and breath by breath Blount measures out his life, trembling in the bloodwater. He seems to feel that he can hear Yancey behind him somewhere, laughing.

Laughing and shouting, impossible curses resounding off the walls and streams . . . but no time for that now, no time for any of it; he feels barely alive now, the precariously placed little Blount, and even the spontaneous arrival of Yancey in full battle regalia—why not? is this more impossible than the events of the Projector themselves?—would not bring him above terror. He is simply no longer a thinking, reasoning little being; his rational powers have been defeated; so has his rhetoric; all that he knows is the desire to be alive to fight another day, and semi-conscious he bounces from level to level, dropping off the plumes of the large intestine and finally through a series of events which happen too rapidly and asymmetrically for the following cameras to capture, through an onset of sheer luck, Blount lands in a small open pocket in the intestine which, in its own severe distress, evacuates him violently and immediately. Blount is expelled through the anus of his dying patient like a shotgun pellet; he slams against a wall but is fortunately of too little mass to find the blow anything but stunning, he collapses off the wall and onto the floor, narrowly missing (although he never would have known it) an open container of alcohol in which he would have disgracefully drowned and lies on the floor then in momentary safety while above him Yancey, *in extremis*, shrieks and pulls on the sheets, heaves on the bed, arises to a penitential posture and hands locked against one another tries to scream out his dying moments. But Yancey cannot scream. His throat is blocked by blood.

And so there is no one to come down these halls; no sound in this room, only the whisking of sheets, the slow grunts of the dying patient, expelling his life now in little moans and bubbles. Blount's terrified little shrieks could not have been heard, the ruination of the blood inside is soundless. Monumental events in short have occurred, are still occurring and no one to bear witness, least of all Blount who is, strictly speaking, insensible on the floor. Yancey's death-dance continues in the shattering quiet; little plastic bottles dance on the bed-shelf. Still there are no sounds to attract observation. The final events, as almost all final events do, occur emptily and in humid scatology. There is very little dignity in all of this.

Thirty-six seconds after Yancey's last moan, the lock of the Projector fails within Blount for the last time and he is reconstituted in size. Conscious or unconscious, life and the wonderful work of the Projector must go on; there is a dull thump and with wiggling and straining, a five foot one inch form appears inertly on the floor, clawing at its eyes, squealing at the pictures of blood it sees.

Gasping, it rises to its feet more unconscious than sane, still unadjusted to its new bulk, mumbling to itself. It runs hysterically toward a wall, still fighting off the blood, hits it full tilt, absorbs the blow on its head and then sinks again to its knees. Blount has been through a very difficult time of it; of this there can be little question.

In the bed Yancey squirrels around, makes one last effort to rise to his feet and then falls back, dead or dying of a series of massive occlusions. Blount does not see this. It is too bad; he has waited on the spectacle for so long, worked toward it with such difficulty that it seems that he would deserve at least to be present at execution. But his condition, although far more medically stable than Yancey's, is nevertheless almost comatose. He does not, therefore, see Yancey dying in the sheets and the fact that he has been robbed of this opportunity may be the full and final explanation as to why his life from that moment forward is so difficult . . .

Or then again it may simply be a continuation of that difficult luck which for twenty-two and a fraction of years has led Blount, almost every moment of every day, to doubt the reality of his own motives.

EPILOGUE

On the floor, in the thirty minutes before the attendants at last checking the hall monitors on Yancey and suspecting something amiss break into the room, in the thirty minutes before the attendants seize Blount, slap him roughly to consciousness and bring him down the hallways for an immediate interrogation, in the half hour before Blount is then formally charged with the murder of Yancey—because the fool, under the quickening influence of some whiskey eased into him by small doses, tells the truth at once—and led through the great subterranean corridors of the Institute to his own stone cell because the Institute has, for twenty years, been its own disciplinary unit, in the half hour before his name is removed from the great seal and rolls of the Institute and his little head is shaved for the execution-as-example, in then the last half hour of his effective life, the unconscious Blount has a deep dream of remission and in this dream Susan appears before him in the room, just after he has committed the murder and embraces him.

It is not the terrified, unconscious Blount of the actual events whom she embraces, but a Blount reconstituted, a Blount transmogrified, who holds her back for all he is worth, feeling the freeing vault and surge in his loins, knowing at last that by the murder he has made himself a man and that now, now he could possess her. She is crying gently into his shoulder. "For me," she says, "you did it for me."

"For you and for us," he says, touching her hair, and

then motions to the corpse on the bed. "And for him as well, the poor damned bastard. It was better this way."

And now she laughs: instead of crying, laughter: a very volatile girl, it seems to run in the family, and Blount draws her against him, feeling her breasts prodding and poking against his chest, feeling an excitement he never has before: yes, that is him, that is Blount with the erection now scraping at her thighs, Blount with the palms floating up and down her shoulders, no one else but the demented little Messenger himself and she is responding. He feels her lips on his cheek; feels them open as her tongue touches him. He casts a look over his shoulder somewhat jarring the contact, reminded suddenly of the corpse.

"Oh don't worry about that," Susan says. "That just makes it more exciting, don't you think? oh it's so terribly exciting."

She comes fully against him now, every pore open: in a dream he opens his mouth and touches her tongue with his own and he is swelling, swelling.

"Beautiful," she is saying. "Beautiful, beautiful," although whether she is talking about what is happening between them or merely commenting on the unfortunate creature in the bed, Blount does not know. Does it matter? Here she is and here he is, at last functioning. Her clothes, in this dream, fall away from her and she is naked against him. He is the same. They are both naked together. His genitals, erected, graze and bob against her thighs; he could enter her now if he wanted. She is cavernous, grasping, he could bury himself within her. Perhaps he will. He will. He will enter her now.

In this dream, half an hour before they burst into the room to take him away for ever, a half an hour before Yancey's corpse, streaming in its vapors and disaster is yanked from the bed to fall like inert plumbing to the floor, in the half hour before Yancey's granddaughter enters upon the scene screaming and has to be carried off shouting that she knows exactly what has happened and she will bring down scandal upon the Institute (she can afford to make a nuisance of herself, she will inherit five million dollars, not a bad price for a little impotent incest) in, then, what is effectively the last half hour of his life, Blount dreams that he enters the girl tumultuously, vaulting and growing within her, scraping her at last to the most secret and hidden parts of herself and everything that he does, every motion incites her to greater and greater response.

"Beautiful," she says, standing, embracing him, throwing her arms around his neck and raising herself slightly so that he can seize a breast in his mouth. "Beautiful, beautiful," and with beauty he parts her, with beauty he surges into her, the ancient strokes of generation overpoweringly fresh to Blount for he has never done this before and he comes quickly, three or four of these strokes and already he is done but as she gasps and climaxes around him, holding his prick like a flower, he casts one eye back toward the bed then and, as he knew he would, sees the dead eye of Yancey peering back at him . . . and with a cry tumbles into that wink, falling densely until finally he has toppled all the way inside Yancey and perched in the gut then like a tiny frog, pulls the blanket of the blood over him . . . and there, shielded from Susan's unheard cries, he rests forever.

CITIES IN FLIGHT: his famous science fiction quartet

James Blish

THEY SHALL HAVE STARS

A.D. 2018 – the Cold Peace, worse even than the Cold War with bureaucratic regimes in Washington and Moscow indistinguishable in their passion for total repression. But in the West, a few dedicated individuals still struggle to find a way out of the trap of human history.

A LIFE FOR THE STARS

The world's natural resources have long been exhausted and city after city goes 'Okie' – lifts off the earth to earn its living among the stars.

EARTHMAN, COME HOME

When the cities left earth, they moved into a constantly changing environment. In a multi-cultural universe an iron hand was needed to impose order upon the spaceways.

A CLASH OF CYMBALS

Earth is finished as a galactic power. Now, from the heart of the Milky Way, come the first tentative strands of the Web of Hercules – the strange culture that is destined to be the next great civilization of the galaxy.